A History of the Christian Tradition

*From Its Jewish Origins
to the Reformation*

Thomas D. McGonigle, O.P.
James F. Quigley, O.P.

PAULIST PRESS
NEW YORK ◆ MAHWAH

Interior artwork and maps by John Davis Gummere

Book design by Nighthawk Design.

Scripture quotations are from the Revised Standard Version Bible, copyright 1946, 1952, 1971 by the Division of Christian Education of the National Council of Churches of Christ in the USA, and are used by permission.

The cutaway illustration of the Dura-Europos house is reprinted from *The Early Christian and Byzantine World* by Jean Lassus, published by the Hamlyn Publishing Group Ltd. and the McGraw-Hill Book Company.

The cover illustration, a Christian figure with orb and scepter from 5th century Egypt, is reproduced by permission of the Brooklyn Museum.

Library of Congress Cataloging-in-Publication Data

McGonigle, Thomas D., 1941–
    A history of the Christian tradition.

    Includes index.
    1. Church history. I. Quigley, James F.,
1938–   . II. Title.
BR162.2.M38 1988   270   87-35975
ISBN 0-8091-2964-7 (pbk.)

Published by Paulist Press
997 Macarthur Boulevard
Mahwah, New Jersey 07430

Printed and bound in the
United States of America

Contents

Contents

Appreciations

The authors thank the many people who have contributed to this work—other scholars, our colleagues and our students. We thank Mrs. Mary Garvey for her secretarial assistance. A special word of thanks is owed Mrs. Sylvia White who typed the various drafts of the manuscript and who offered the authors constant encouragement.

We dedicate this book to our parents and families who have been for us the first and the best teachers of the Christian tradition.

1

In the Beginning

There is a story told about a rabbi in the Warsaw ghetto during the Second World War. Every day this official would walk down the street, into the synagogue, up into the pulpit, and say: "Master of the universe, we are here!" Time passed and the ferocity of Nazism was especially unleashed against the Warsaw ghetto in Poland. Still, every day the rabbi would walk down the street, go into the synagogue, step up into the pulpit and say: "Master of the universe, we are here!" The atrocities continued until the rabbi was one of the last Jews left in the ghetto. Still, every day he would sneak down the street, into the synagogue and up into the pulpit. Finally one day he stepped into the pulpit and said: "Master of the universe, as you can see, even now we are still here—but where are you?"

The terrible pain of the holocaust challenges the Jewish people and all peoples on many different levels, not the least of which is the theological level. The Jewish understanding of God is the inheritance of Western civilization. Who then are these people? What is it that binds Jews together? How does their story begin? What is significant in that story?

Who Are the Jewish People?

We use the word "Hebrew" for a certain people living in the Ancient Near East. Some scholars suggest that the word "Hebrew" is derived from the word "apiru," which refers to a group of nomadic Semitic people.

The words "Israel" and "Israelite" also came to denote the Hebrew people. The name "Israel" was given by God to the patriarch Jacob: " . . . and God said to him: Your name is Jacob; no longer shall your name be called Jacob, but Israel shall be your name" (Gen 35:10).

Another word for the Hebrew people is "Jews" or "Jewish." After the reign of King Solomon the kingdom of the Hebrews was split into the northern kingdom of Israel and the southern kingdom of Judah. It is from the latter that we get the word "Jew."

Finally another word used to describe the land of Israel is "Palestine." Throughout the twelfth and eleventh centuries B.C.E. the threat to Israel was increased by the pressure of newcomers known as Philistines. The Philistines were one of a number of "Sea Peoples" who poured out of the Aegean Sea onto the eastern shores of the Mediterranean. It was from these people that Canaan, the land promised by God to the Hebrews, later received the name "Palestine." The Greek form of the name "Philistine" became the Roman term for the land of Canaan—"Palestina," in English "Palestine."

What Binds the Jewish People Together?

The identity of the Jewish people and that which binds them together is the holy word of God as found in the Bible. The Bible is also the principal source for the story of the Jewish people. Jewish people always speak about the "Hebrew" Bible while Christian people refer to that collection of documents as the "Old Testament." There are twenty-four books in the Hebrew Bible which are divided differently by Protestants and Roman Catholics. Protestants count thirty-nine books in the Old Testament while Roman Catholics count forty-six books. The word "Bible" comes from the Greek words *ta biblia* meaning "the books."

PENTATEUCH OR TORAH	GENESIS
	EXODUS
	LEVITICUS
	NUMBERS
	DEUTERONOMY
HISTORICAL BOOKS	JOSHUA
	JUDGES
	RUTH
	1 and 2 SAMUEL
	1 and 2 KINGS

	1 and 2 CHRONI- CLES EZRA NEHEMIAH	
	ESTHER	
	JUDITH* *TOBIT* *BARUCH* *1 and 2 MACCA-* *BEES*	Included in the Catholic Bible be- cause found in the Greek "Septuagint."
WISDOM WRITING	JOB PSALMS PROVERBS ECCLESIASTES SONG OF SONGS	
	ECCLESIASTICUS *WISDOM OF* *SOLOMON*	
PROPHETS		
Major Prophets:	ISAIAH JEREMIAH LAMENTATIONS EZEKIEL (DANIEL)	
Minor Prophets	HOSEA JOEL AMOS OBADIAH JONAH MICAH	NAHUM HABAKKUK ZEPHANIAH HAGGAI ZECHARIAH MALACHI

*Books that are italicized are found only in Catholic Bibles.

The Hebrew Bible (Old Testament) is a collection of documents or works written by different authors for different purposes with different communities in mind over a period of one thousand years and employing a whole host of different literary forms. The Hebrew Bible began to be put into writing in the ninth century B.C.E. When authors spoke of the ancient past or history of the early Jews they wrote what they received through oral traditions. These traditions had passed on from father to son, mother to daughter, over the centuries—traditions which spoke of the origins of the Hebrew people and of God's great interventions in their history.

The Bible, especially in reference to the ancient history of the Jewish people, is the chief source—often the only source—of our knowledge for that history. What is read in the Hebrew Bible is a theological history of the Jewish people. What happened to them is seen through the lens of religion. The events, the joys and sorrows of a people, are all viewed as through a screen or grid which is the religion of the Hebrews. God is understood as acting directly in the history of his chosen people. What happens to them is no accident or the effect of some whimsical power but rather the will of God for his people.

The Bible is seen by religious people as a holy and sacred book. It is not simply a source of history or a product of human ingenuity and imagination. Jews and Christians alike believe it is the revealed word of God.

How Does the Jewish Story Begin?

The Book of Genesis contains a description of the ancient history of the Hebrew people. In Egypt, while in slavery, the people looked back in time and understood themselves to be connected to a Semitic people who had not always lived in Egypt. While their present plight was that of slavery, it had not always been so. The Hebrews in Egypt saw themselves vaguely connected both on an ethnic level and on a religious level with patriarchs or fathers—Abraham, Isaac, Jacob and Joseph. God had first revealed himself to Abraham and established a covenant with him.

> After these things the word of the Lord came to Abram in a vision, "Fear not, Abram, I am your shield; your reward shall be very great." And he brought him outside and said, "Look toward heaven, and number the stars, if you are able to number them." Then he said to him, "So shall your descendants be." And he believed the Lord; and he reckoned it to him as righteousness. On that day the Lord made a covenant with Abram, saying, "To your

3500 BCE	3000	2200–2000	2000–1750
Sumerian civilization	Bronze Age Gilgamesh epic	Egyptian pyramids	Middle Kingdom of Egypt

descendants I give this land, from the river of Egypt to the great river, the river Euphrates" (Gen 15:1, 5–6, 18).

God promised Abraham that he would be the father of a great nation. He also promised that he would lead Abraham to a promised land—a land of milk and honey.

The covenant with Abraham was renewed with Isaac and later again with Jacob.

> And the Lord appeared to him, and said, "Do not go down to Egypt; dwell in the land of which I shall tell you. Sojourn in this land, and I will be with you, and I will bless you; for to you and your descendants I will give all these lands, and I will fulfill the oath which I swore to Abraham your father. I will multiply your descendants as the stars of heaven, and will give to your descendants all these lands; and by your descendants all the nations of the earth shall bless themselves: because Abraham obeyed my commandments, my statutes, and my laws" (Gen 26:2–5).

Thus did God renew his covenant with Isaac. Again to Isaac's son Jacob we hear God speak:

> Jacob left Beer-sheba, and went toward Haran. And he came to a certain place, and stayed there that night, because the sun had set. Taking one of the stones of the place, he put it under his head and lay down in that place to sleep. And he dreamed that there was a ladder set up on the earth, and the top of it reached to heaven; and behold, the angels of God were ascending and decending on it! And behold, the Lord stood above it and said, "I am the Lord, the God of Abraham your father and the God of Isaac; the land on which you lie I will give to you and to your descendants; and your descendants shall be like the dust of the earth, and you shall spread abroad to the west and to the east and to the north and to the south; and by you and your descendants shall all the families of the earth bless themselves" (Gen 28:10–14).

The story continues with Moses, detailed in the Book of Exodus, the second book of the Bible. Moses was a Hebrew, born in Egypt and

1700	1550–1150	1378
Babylonian Empire; Shang Dynasty in China	New Kingdom in Egypt	Monotheism in Egypt

1800–1300 BCE
Patriarchal period

brought up at the Egyptian court. In adulthood he identified himself with his own people. The Exodus story tells us that Moses, while attempting to defend a Hebrew slave, killed a chief of a labor battalion. Because of this Moses eventually was forced to flee to the desert. There he joined a nomadic tribe and later married.

At some point Moses experienced God who appeared to him in a burning bush, revealing his divine identity. He called Moses to be an instrument in the deliverance or liberation of the Hebrew people from the power of Egypt. Moses reluctantly accepted this call and with Aaron, his brother, attempted unsuccessfully to convince both the Hebrew people and the Egyptian ruler (pharaoh) that God wished his people to be released so that they might serve him.

> And now, behold, the cry of the people of Israel has come to me, and I have seen the oppression with which the Egyptians oppress them. Come, I will send you to Pharaoh that you may bring forth my people, the sons of Israel, out of Egypt (Ex 3:9–10).

The key foundational event in the Hebrew story was the exodus or the liberation of the Hebrews. Various catastrophic events occurred in Egypt which finally led Pharaoh to permit Moses to leave with the Hebrews. The crucial event was the last of the so-called ten plagues wherein finally the first-born of the Egyptians died. The Hebrews, however, were spared the wrath of the angel of death who "passed over" Hebrew homes. Finally, Pharaoh permitted Moses to lead the Hebrew people through one of the border lakes–the famous Red Sea–narrowly escaping disaster at the hands of pursuing Egyptian troops.

It was after the exodus and in the desert that this nomadic people, the *apiru* or Hebrews, the Israelites or people of the land of Israel, the people of Palestine, became truly a religious community. Through Moses God established a covenant with the Hebrew people. At Mount Sinai God gave Moses the law or Torah. God promised to be faithful to his chosen people, pledging his presence with them as well as land of milk and honey.

Moses did not live to see his people enter into the promised land. Rather it was under Joshua, the successor of Moses and first of the "judges" (*shofet* in Hebrew meaning charismatic leader), that the Hebrew people began their history in the promised land. The history of the Jewish people was a covenantal history—I will be your God and you will be my people. Abraham and his descendants had been nomadic peoples organized in clans. These groups of semi-related peoples came together only as a religious community at the time of the exodus and Sinai revelation. Later on these groups of peoples became a kind of tribal confederacy and settled in the land of Canaan. Later still these tribes became a nation.

The Significance of Moses

Moses was a prophet. A prophet is not a teller of the future nor a predictor of things to come. Neither is a prophet simply a person filled with religious indignation. Rather a prophet is one who has the task of nurturing, nourishing and evoking a consciousness and perception alternative to the consciousness and perception of the dominant culture. A prophet is the voice of God, one who speaks in the place of God.

A prophet challenges the dominant consciousness by rejecting the present ordering of things. At the same time a true prophet not only challenges but also energizes by promising another time and situation, offering a newness which is God's promise. Moses, therefore, was the prophet of God, challenging and energizing.

The God of Moses was different from any other God or gods that other people believed in. Moses' God was a terribly holy God, distant yet near, not an anthropomorphic projection. There was always resistance among the Hebrews to a human representation of God. The Hebrew God was underived and not born; this God had no consort or female counterpart. The religion of Moses was in effect a break with the dominant polytheistic religious style of the time. God was one and only one who, nevertheless, created the world and related intimately to human communities.

Moses spoke to the people of an alternative community, an alternative vision of God and the human person, an alternative way of living. Moses' vision of God, his understanding of the God who had revealed himself, was that God was a God of freedom and new beginnings. This was in contradistinction to the pantheon of Egyptian gods, all of whom existed to justify the status quo. Pharaoh was the divine presence on earth and Egyptian gods blessed and encouraged the static world view and system of Pharaonic Egypt.

The God of Moses promoted a political order based on justice and compassion. Moses spoke of a new way of being a human person. This was in contradistinction to the Egyptian system based on oppression and exploitation. God said to Moses: "I have heard the cries of my people." Moses, the prophet, spoke to the people of an alternative community.

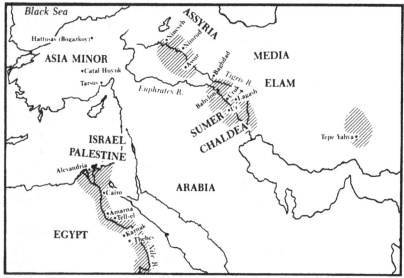

Cradles of Civilization

Historical Setting

The Bible provides us with the story of the Jewish people from the perspective of their perception of themselves as a people called into a covenant relationship with God. From a non-biblical, historical perspective, how does one account for the formation of the Hebrew people?

Around 1780 B.C.E. the fourteenth Egyptian dynasty fell before a group of invading Semitic people who have come to be known as the Hyksos. The fifteenth dynasty, that of the Hyksos (1678–1570 B.C.E.), was probably the period in which the patriarch Joseph and his fellow Semites emigrated from Canaan and eventually came into prominence and favor in Egypt.

When the native Egyptians regained power and established the new kingdom (ca. 1570 B.C.E.), the Hebrews who were associated with the hated Hyksos were reduced to a state of bondage. Sometime in the thirteenth century, perhaps during the reign of Ramses II (1290–1224 B.C.E), the oppressed Hebrews managed to escape from Egypt and flee to Canaan.

Around 1200 B.C.E. the whole of the Middle East experienced a cataclysmic shift in the centers of structured power. The established empires in Egypt, Anatolia (modern Turkey) and Mesopotamia collapsed before the onslaught of an invasion of peoples who have come to be called the "Sea Peoples." Their identity for historians is still something of a mystery. They probably came from the north and east of Anatolia because they had developed iron weapons. The bronze weapons of the Egyptians, the Hittites and the Kassites were no match for them. The breakup of these great empires made possible the emergence of smaller political entities such as the Phoenicians, the Philistines (who were probably themselves a Sea People) and the Hebrews.

The emergence of the Hebrew people as a nation took place at a time when the great powers of the ancient world were in disarray. The power vacuum that existed between 1200 and 800 B.C.E. allowed diverse peoples such as the Hebrews to emerge on the stage of history and establish their national identity in a specific geographical locality.

2

Judges, Kings and Prophets

The Judges

Under the leadership of Moses a diversified group of nomadic people came together around a common belief in the God whose name was revealed in the exodus experience. Moses died however before these people moved into the promised land of Canaan. Under Joshua, Moses' successor, the people entered Canaan and began the conquest of its inhabitants. During the two hundred year period of the "tribal confederacy" leadership was in the hands of certain charismatic figures called judges (in Hebrew, *shofet*).

Since the Hebrew people were often under attack from different quarters, the judges were primarily charismatic military leaders. The famous story of Joshua and the walls of Jericho tumbling down represents the Jewish understanding of the role of the judges. Gideon, Deborah and Samson are examples of other judges who emerged in times of need throughout this period.

> Whenever the Lord raised up judges for them, the Lord was with the judge, and he saved them from the hand of their enemies all the days of the judge; for the Lord was moved to pity by their groaning because of those who afflicted and oppressed them. But whenever the judge died, they turned back and behaved worse than their fathers, going after other gods, serving them and bowing down to them; they did not drop any of their practices or their stubborn ways (Jgs 2:18–19).

The judges also performed a quasi-religious function. They called the people to a renewed awareness of their covenant relationship with God. In turn the people renewed their treaty with God when they responded to the judges' call. They ritualized this commitment to the God of the covenant by offering animal sacrifices at various shrines throughout the land such as Bethel or Shechem.

Major Judges of Ancient Israel

Othniel	Judges 3:7–11
Ehud	Judges 3:12–30
Deborah and Barak	Judges 4:1–5:31
Gideon	Judges 6:1–8:35
Jephthah	Judges 11:1–12:7
Samson	Judges 13:1–16:31

Toward the end of this period, the Philistines, a strong and capable sea-faring people, landed on the shores of Palestine. Because they used iron to make weapons and tools, the Philistines became a formidable opponent to the Hebrew people. From their established cities on the Palestinian coast, they moved toward the interior of the country. The military threat of the Philistines provided the impetus for the Hebrew people to approach the last of the judges, Samuel. When they asked him to anoint a king, Samuel rebuked the people for their request because in the Hebrew universe there could be only one true king, God. For the judges, Israel was a theocratic political entity. Samuel said that the people would regret the day when they asked for a king. He warned them:

These will be the ways of the king who will reign over you; he will take your sons and appoint them to his chariots and to be his horsemen. He will take your daughters to be perfumers and cooks and bakers. He will take the best of your fields and vineyards and olive orchards and give them to his servants. And in that day you will cry out because of your king, whom you have chosen for yourselves; but the Lord will not answer you in that day (1 Sam 8:11, 13–14, 18).

The Kings

The Hebrew monarchy lasted a little over four hundred years (1020–587 B.C.E.). During this time Israel reached the heights of its influence in the Ancient Near East, and achieved a great deal of power as well as eventually sinking into the pit of corruption and despair.

The Kings of Israel and Judah

Saul   1020–1000 B.C.E.
David   1000–961
Solomon   961–929

Kings of Israel	Kings of Judah
Jeroboam 929–910	Rehoboam 929–913
Nadab 910–909	Abijah 913–911
Baasha 909–886	Asa 911–871
Elah 886–885	Jehoshaphat 871–850
Zimri 885	Joram 850–843
Tibni 885–881	Ahaziah 843
Omri 885–874	Athaliah 842–836
Ahab 874–851	Jehoash 836–803
Ahaziah 851–850	Amaziah 803–775
Joram 850–842	Azariah 775–734
Jehu 842–820	Jotham 734–733
Jehoahaz 820–804	Ahaz 733–714
Joash 804–789	Hezekiah 714–696
Jeroboam II 789–748	Manasseh 696–642
Zechariah 748	Amon 641–640
Menahem 748–736	Josiah 639–609
Pekahiah 736–735	Joahaz 609
Pekah 735–732	Jehoiakim 608–598
Hoshea 732–721	Jehoiachin 598–597
	Zedekiah 597–587

Saul

The first king of the Hebrews, Saul (1020–1000 B.C.E.), was a military leader recognized by the various Jewish tribes. Saul was a king who had a traveling court, a tent residence, little money and no slaves. He was a simple man with a single purpose—to expel the Philistines from the land of Israel. While Saul and his son Jonathan accomplished many military exploits, he felt betrayed and threatened by David, a former shepherd, who had joined his army. The complexity of Saul, who was a good man troubled by mental anguish described as "an evil spirit from God" (1 Sam 16:15), especially revealed itself in his checkered relationship with David. As the first king of Israel, Saul was a great leader and a firm believer in God, yet finally his accomplishments were torn apart by his own interior or mental darkness.

> Then Samuel said to Saul, "Why have you disturbed me by bringing me up?" Saul answered, "I am in great distress; for the Philistines are warring against me, and God has turned away from me and answers me no more, either by prophets or by dreams; therefore I have summoned you to tell me what I shall do." And Samuel said, "Why then do you ask me, since the Lord has turned from you and become your enemy? The Lord has done this to you as he spoke by me; for the Lord has torn the kingdom out of your hand, and given it to your neighbor, David" (1 Sam 28:15–17).

David

Saul was succeeded by David (1000–961 B.C.E.), one of the most significant figures in the Hebrew story. As a soldier, an administrator and a religious leader, David formed Israel into a powerful kingdom built on a dynastic rule. After succeeding to the throne, David captured the city of Jerusalem and made it the capital of the united kingdom formed out of the old confederacy of the twelve tribes of Israel and the subsequent weak political entity ruled by Saul.

David built a palace in Jerusalem as a place of assembly for his family and for the royal court. Here he centralized the worship of the God of the covenant as the God of the nation of Israel. Under David's rule, Israelite influence expanded and the nation achieved the pinnacle of political greatness, becoming the leading power of the eastern end of the Mediterranean.

> When David's time to die drew near, he charged Solomon his son, saying, "I am about to go the way of all the earth. Be strong, and show yourself a man, and keep the charge of the Lord your God, walking in his ways and keeping his statutes, his commandments, his ordinances, and his testimonies, as it is written in the law of Moses, that you may prosper in all that you do and wherever you turn; that the Lord may establish his word which he spoke concerning me, saying, "If your sons take heed to their way, to walk before me in faithfulness with all their heart and with all their soul,

there shall not fail you a man on the throne of Israel" (1 Kings 2:1–4).

Solomon

Solomon (961–929 B.C.E.), who was reputed to be one of the wisest men in history, succeeded his father David. While Solomon's fame may be deserved, it is also true that he was a pampered son who lived in a world of luxury far removed from the experience of ordinary people. Solomon amassed and dispensed great wealth, thus encouraging ostentation and display.

Solomon began extensive building projects, his most noted achievement being the construction of the first temple in Jerusalem, which became the center of Jewish religious life. However, he also permitted other religions and the worship of foreign gods. To pay for his way of life and his building projects, Solomon taxed his people and introduced slavery. His accomplishments were extraordinary but they also provoked deep division within his realm, especially in the northern section of the kingdom.

When Solomon had finished building the house of the Lord and the king's house and all that Solomon desired to build, the Lord appeared to Solomon a second time, as he had appeared to him at Gibeon. And the Lord said to him, "I have heard your prayer and supplication, which you have made before me; I have consecrated this house which you have built, and put my name there for ever;

Solomon's Temple

my eyes and my heart will be there for all time. And as for you, if you will walk before me, as David your father walked, with integrity of heart and uprightness, doing according to all that I have commanded you, and keeping my statutes and ordinances, then I will establish your royal throne over Israel for ever, as I promised David your father, saying, 'There shall not fail you a man upon the throne of Israel.' But if you turn aside from following me, you or your children, and do not keep my commandments and statutes which I have set before you, but go and serve other gods and worship them, then I will cut off Israel from the land which I have given them; and the house which I have consecrated for my name I will cast out of my sight; and Israel will become a proverb and a byword among all peoples. And this house will become a heap of ruins" (1 Kgs 9:1–8).

The Northern and Southern Kingdoms

After the reign of Solomon marked by materialism, economic depletion, suspension of tribal and personal freedoms, sensuality, religious syncretism and favoritism for the south, the stage was set for political division. The northern part of the kingdom broke away from the south and became the independent kingdom of Israel between 929 and 721 B.C.E. The first king of Israel, Jeroboam (929–910 B.C.E.), strove to break the emotional and religious ties with Jerusalem by setting up a new religious center at Bethel. Tension, conflict and religious struggle between the northern and southern kingdoms ended tumultuously in 721 B.C.E. when the Assyrians conquered Israel and sent many of its inhabitants into exile. The Jews who remained eventually intermarried with the pagan immigrants sent by the Assyrians to the region as colonists. This half-breed population would in time become the Samaritans living in isolation and alienation from the mainstream of Judaism.

The kingdom of Judah, the southern portion of the formerly unified kingdom, was able to maintain its identity through religious compromise, political treaties and a precarious balancing act between the great powers of the Middle East, Assyria and Egypt, until 587 B.C.E. In that year, the Babylonians, the new power in the mideast that had conquered Assyria and succeeded to its empire in the person of King Nebuchadnezzar, destroyed Jerusalem and its temple. The survivors of the destruction of the city of David went into exile in Babylon where they would be purified in their faith as they waited for the opportunity to return to the promised land.

Monarchy in Hebrew history had ambiguous results. It is true that under their kings Israel was able to move from being simply a group of tribes vaguely related around a common God to being a nation. Under their kings the Hebrew people and the Hebrew nation achieved a certain degree of political and economic power in the Ancient Near East. The monarchy, however, traded off its commitment to the covenant for worldly power and possessions. The temptation for Hebrew men and women, whenever they related to the wider world of the surrounding cultures, was to surrender their own integrity as a people covenanted to and with God.

Gradually during the period of the monarchy, Israel moved away from Moses' vision of an alternative community. Slowly Israel's commitment both to a free God and to a policy of justice and freedom corroded. By the end of Solomon's reign, Israel was beginning to lose its identity as an alternative community. It began to approach the Egyptian model—a nation which believed in a static god undergirding the status quo politically and economically and a nation which maintained a regimen of injustice and oppression.

The Two Kingdoms

During the monarchy and especially during the age of the divided kingdoms, individual religious figures rose up to challenge the dominant culture and value system adopted by the Jewish people. These charismatic individuals, the prophets, called for renewal and conversion and warned Israel of the impending disaster which would come from God as a just punishment for their evil actions.

The Prophets of Ancient Israel and Judah

Amos	(c. 750 B.C.E.)
Hosea	(c. 745 B.C.E.)
Isaiah	(c. 742–700 B.C.E.)
Micah	(c. 722–701 B.C.E.)
Zephaniah	(c. 628–622 B.C.E.)
Jeremiah	(c. 626–587 B.C.E.)
Nahum	(c. 612 B.C.E.)
Habakkuk	(c. 605 B.C.E.)
Ezekiel	(c. 593–573 B.C.E.)
Obadiah	(after 587 B.C.E.)
Deutero-Isaiah	(c. 540 B.C.E.)
Haggai	(c. 520–515 B.C.E.)
Zechariah	(c. 520–515 B.C.E.)
Joel	(c. 500–350 B.C.E.)
Malachi	(c. 500–450 B.C.E.)

The Prophets

The prophets were not soothsayers. Rather, they were spokespersons for issues affecting the divine-human relationship between God and the people of Israel. They were deeply religious figures or mystics whose lives manifested that God was always passionately at the center of their vision. Called and chosen by God for a particular task, the prophets were sent to the people with a particular message for the present moment of history. Prophets spoke both on religious and political matters, rejecting foreign idolatries and urging resistance to foreign domination. In their denunciation of idolatry and the politics of injustice, they spoke for God by calling people back to the covenant.

At the same time, the prophets not only challenged but also ener-

gized. They offered the vision of new possibilities by calling the Hebrew people back to the ideals of the alternative community at the
heart of the exodus experience. The vision of a deliverer or a great
liberator emerged gradually within the prophetic tradition. One
would come who would save Israel from its suffering and sorrow. A
new people would be born through the work of this great Messiah, a
people renewed in their covenantal relationship with God.

Amos

Prophets emerged in both the northern and southern kingdoms. In
the north two very significant figures were the prophets Amos (c.
750 B.C.E.) and Hosea (c. 745 B.C.E.). Amos consistently reminded
Israel of its special relationship with God. That relationship, however, was not a privilege but a responsibility. The God of Israel was
the God of all nations, and Israel's role was to recognize that truth.
Amos called the people to repent of their idolatry and injustice.

> Seek good, and not evil, that you may live; and so the Lord, the God
> of hosts, will be with you, as you have said. Hate evil, and love good,
> and establish justice in the gate; it may be that the Lord, the God of
> hosts, will be gracious to the remnant of Joseph (Am 5:14–15).

Hosea

Within the northern kingdom, the prophet Hosea called for repentance. He poetically compared the covenant between God and his
people to a marriage. As Hosea's wife became a harlot, so too Israel
had become a harlot. Just as Hosea, because of love and tenderness,
wills to accept his wife back, so too God, because of *hesed* (tender
mercy and steadfast love), is willing to receive Israel back after she
had become unfaithful to God by accepting local Canaanite deities.
For Hosea, God is love.

> And in that day, says the Lord, you will call me, "My husband" and
> no longer will you call me, "My Baal." ... And I will betroth you to

	1250 Destruction of Troy			
1290 Moses and the Exodus	1200–1220 The Judges		1000–961 King David	961–922 King Solomon

me for ever; I will betroth you to me in righteousness and in justice, in steadfast love, and in mercy. I will betroth you to me in faithfulness; and you shall know the Lord (Hos 2:18, 21–22).

Isaiah

A number of prophets arose in the southern kingdom prior to the exile (587 B.C.E.), during the exile (586–538 B.C.E.), and after the return to Judah. Two of the foremost of the prophets within the southern kingdom were Isaiah (742–700 B.C.E.) and Jeremiah (626–587 B.C.E.). For Isaiah, God was king of all peoples, and most holy. He was also judge of the broken covenant who would punish the chosen people in order to bring them to repentance. God would not leave his people without hope, but would send Immanuel as a deliverer or liberator to free his people.

For a child is born to us, a son is given to us; and the government will be upon his shoulder, and his name will be called "Wonderful Counselor, Mighty God, Everlasting Father, Prince of Peace." Of the increase of his government and of peace there will be no end, upon the throne of David, and over his kingdom, to establish it, and to uphold it with justice and with righteousness from this time forth and for evermore. The zeal of the Lord of hosts will do this (Is 9:6–7).

Jeremiah

Jeremiah portrayed God's purpose as healing a broken relationship. He recalled the faith of Moses and spoke of the need for personal faith. Individuals and the community needed to undergo conversion. Only then would a new beginning be possible and would Israel be able to emerge anew as an alternative community.

Behold, the days are coming, says the Lord, when I will make a new covenant with the house of Israel and the house of Judah, not like the covenant which I made with their fathers when I took them by the hand to bring them out of the land of Egypt, my

	753			660	
	Rome founded			Japanese emperors	
922–721	922–586	750/745	742–700	626–587	586
Judah	Israel	Amos/Hosea	Isaiah	Jeremiah	Jerusalem
The Divided Kingdom					falls

covenant which they broke, though I was their husband, says the Lord. But this is the covenant which I will make with the house of Israel after those days, says the Lord: I will put my law within them, and I will write it upon their hearts; and I will be their God, and they shall be my people. And no longer shall each man teach his neighbor and each his brother, saying, Know the Lord, for they shall all know me, from the least of them to the greatest, says the Lord; for I will forgive their iniquity, and I will remember their sin no more (Jer 31:31–34).

The prophets spoke to a people about their fundamental identity. The Hebrew people were precisely who they were because of God's choice of them as a people with whom he would establish a covenant. They lived that covenant by observing the law or Torah. The prophets were religious leaders sent by God to recall the people to the covenant relationship which was the source of their identity. The Hebrew people were to be an alternative community, challenging the status quo of the dominant culture. They were to have a unique vision of God as well as a unique vision of what it meant to be a human person. The prophets reminded the people of Moses' initial intuition and called them to recapture that view. Some listened to the prophets as they challenged and energized while others rejected their message. Both the north and the south experienced the divine punishment for unfaithfulness. The northern kingdom was destroyed in 721 B.C.E. by the Assyrians, and the southern kingdom fell before the power of the Babylonians in 587 B.C.E. Jerusalem and the temple were no more. The people lived in exile far from the promised land of the covenant.

By the waters of Babylon, there we sat down and wept, when we remembered Zion. On the willows there we hung up our lyres. For there our captors required of us songs, and our tormentors, mirth, saying, "Sing us one of the songs of Zion!" How shall we sing the Lord's song in a foreign land? If I forget you, O Jerusalem, let my right hand wither! Let my tongue cleave to the roof of my mouth, if I do not remember you, if I do not set Jerusalem above my highest joy (Ps 137:1–6).

3

The Exile and After

The Exile

After 721 B.C.E. the Jewish people were those who lived in the kingdom of Judah. In 597 B.C.E. the Babylonian king, Nebuchadnezzar, laid siege to Jerusalem and carried off the leading citizens to Babylon on the distant Euphrates River. Ten years later, in 587 B.C.E., he commenced a final onslaught against the citizens of Judah. The city and the temple built by Solomon were destroyed and the people were sent into exile to Babylon. Some Jews, mostly peasants, remained on the land in Judah; others went south to Egypt. This marks the beginning of the Jewish "diaspora," a word meaning "dispersed." Jews had begun to be "dispersed" throughout the known world.

Babylon was a magnificent city and one of the wonders of the ancient world. Many different schools of thought and religious world views flourished within its walls. This environment of pagan worship and economic affluence confronted the Jews in Babylon as never before with a culture that threatened their faith. During their approximately forty years of exile some Jews did succumb to the pressures of the dominant culture and embraced other gods; many did not. To preserve their religion and life-style while in exile the Jewish people redefined their way of being Jewish.

The temple of Solomon had come to be the central place for Jewish worship before the exile. People made pilgrimage to the temple to offer sacrifice and the priests, through their multiple temple offices, cared for the religious needs of the people. Now in exile the situation was very different. The temple had been destroyed, and the previous forms of worship and religious ministry were no longer possible. Where would the people worship and how?

The prophets had paved the way when they insisted that God was present in all of the world and not just in the holy of holies within the temple. During the exile the Jewish people gathered together in small groups to reflect upon and study God's word as expressed in the law (Torah) and to worship. This form of meeting for study and prayer became the "synagogue," which literally means "gathering together." This change in the worship life of the Jewish people necessitated a new class of priests, the Levites, a cadre of teaching priests who were distinct from the ritual or sacrificial priests. The Levites understood their religious duties as studying the law and ancient traditions and commenting on them in writing. This major shift in their religious life caused the remnant of Jews in exile to understand their faith and to practice it on a new and deeper level than before.

The Return from Exile

In 538 B.C.E. a new political power, Persia, rose to dominance, guided by the brilliant leadership of one man, Cyrus (550–530 B.C.E.). Cyrus was an enlightened ruler whose philosophy of governance included a profound respect for the variety of religious traditions within the Persian empire. And so with the blessing of Cyrus, after forty-eight years of exile, a group of Jews returned to the land of Israel. Not all Jews, however, did return to their homeland. Some chose to stay on in Babylon, becoming part of the great diaspora experience of the Hebrew people.

In 520 B.C.E. the Jews rebuilt the temple of Solomon and began anew to become a people with a national political identity. The Jews in Israel, however, lived a precarious existence, for they had to cope with their status as subjects of the Persian empire and to provide for their needs in a land that was poor and required a great deal of work. As always the men and women of Israel were faced with the challenge of maintaining their faith amid the threats of other cultures and other religious world views.

539	509		336–323
Babylon falls	Roman republic	Plato	Alexander
587–538	515	445	325–198
Babylonian captivity	Temple rebuilt	Nehemiah	Egypt rules Palestine

Post-Exilic Judaism

Nehemiah

The words of Nehemiah the son of Hacaliah. Now it happened in the month of Chislev, in the twentieth year, as I was in Susa the capital, that Hanani, one of my brethren, came with certain men out of Judah; and I asked them concerning the Jews that survived, who had escaped exile, and concerning Jerusalem. And they said to me, "The survivors there in the province who escaped exile are in great trouble and shame; the wall of Jerusalem is broken down, and its gates are destroyed by fire."

Now I was cupbearer to the king. In the month of Nisan, in the twentieth year of King Artaxerxes, when wine was before him, I took up the wine and gave it to the king. Now I had not been sad in his presence. And the king said to me, "Why is your face sad, seeing you are not sick? This is nothing else but sadness of the heart." Then I was very much afraid. I said to the king, "Let the king live for ever! Why should not my face be sad, when the city, the place of my fathers' sepulchres, lies waste, and its gates have been destroyed by fire?" Then the king said to me, "For what do you make request?" So I prayed to the God of heaven. And I said to the king, "If it pleases the king, and if your servant has found favor in your sight, that you send me to Judah, to the city of my fathers' sepulchres, that I may rebuild it." And the king said to me (the queen sitting beside him), "How long will you be gone, and when will you return?" So it pleased the king to send me; and I set him a time (Neh 1:1–3, 11c; 2:1–6).

In 445 B.C.E. the Persians sent a Jew named Nehemiah from Babylon to govern the people of Israel. In the course of his rule this enlightened Nehemiah instituted reforms designed to bind the Jews closely into a tight-knit community. To insure Jewish identity he prohibited intermarriage with non-Jews so that membership in the Jewish community was by birth alone. In the area of religious prac-

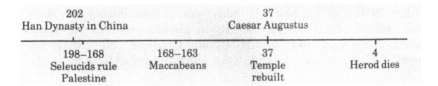

202		37	
Han Dynasty in China		Caesar Augustus	
198–168	168–163	37	4
Seleucids rule Palestine	Maccabeans	Temple rebuilt	Herod dies

tice Nehemiah struggled to preserve the identity of the people and the distinctiveness of Israel's faith amid other cultures by enforcing a strict observance of the sabbath and calling for loyalty to Torah and support of the temple. He also rebuilt the walls of Jerusalem in order to insure the possibility of defense.

Ezra

And all the people gathered as one man into the square before the Water Gate; and they told Ezra the scribe to bring the book of the law of Moses which the Lord had given to Israel. And Ezra the priest brought the law before the assembly, both men and women and all who could hear with understanding, on the first day of the seventh month. And he read from it facing the square before the Water Gate from early morning until mid-day, in the presence of the men and women and those who could understand; and the ears of all the people were attentive to the book of the law. . . .

And Nehemiah, who was the governor, and Ezra the priest and scribe, and the Levites said to all the people, "This day is holy to the Lord your God; do not mourn or weep." For all the people wept when they heard the words of the law. . . .

And all the people went their way to eat and drink and to send portions and to make great rejoicing, because they had understood the words that were spoken to them (Neh 8:1–3, 9, 12).

Some years after Nehemiah began his second term as governor (428 B.C.E.) Ezra, the priest, came from Babylon. On one of the great Jewish festal days, the feast of Tabernacles, Ezra renewed the covenant by reading the book of the law to the people. Ezra's contribution was that he re-established the Pentateuch or the first five books of the Bible, the books of the law, as the basis of Jewish faith and practice. Because of this reform, in conformity with the law, he is called the "father" of Judaism. Since living according to the Torah was the hallmark of fidelity to oneself and to the covenant, it was absolutely necessary to know and interpret the law.

Jewish life as we know it today was defined during the post-exilic period. The basis for identity as always was the covenantal relationship with God: "I will be your God and you will be my people." That covenant was lived out on the practical level by obedi-

Facade of the Rebuilt Temple

ence to law. The law or Torah was not a dead word but rather one
that developed over time through interpretation. The written interpretations of the law became the Mishna. Subsequent commentaries and interpretations, written down, on the Torah and Mishna
became the Talmud.

In the post-exilic period the temple had been rebuilt and ritual
sacrifice conducted by the priests on behalf of the people again became an important mode of worshiping God. However, parallel to
the temple and its priesthood, and coming out of the experience of
the exile, the synagogue, with its teaching priesthood also became a
significant institution in the religious life of the people of Israel.
There the Jewish people reflected on, studied and interpreted Torah.

The Hellenistic Era

In 334 B.C.E. the ancient world began a new phase of its development when the brilliant young general from Macedonia, Alexander
the Great, moved into Asia. In 332 B.C.E. he conquered Palestine.
At Alexander's death in 323 B.C.E. his empire was divided among
his generals. At first the Ptolemies of Egypt ruled Judah; they were
succeeded in 198 B.C.E. by the Seleucid dynasty of Syria. In 195
B.C.E. the Seleucid leader, Antiochus Epiphanes, succeeded to the
throne. This despotic leader outlawed the Jewish religion by ordering Torah or the books of the law to be burned and by forbidding
circumcision and worship on the sabbath. The temple of Jerusalem
was desecrated by pagan altars and sacrifices and an idolatrous
statue of Zeus—the famous "abomination of desolation."

The issue during this period was one familiar to the Jewish people. It was the question of faith and culture. How does one preserve
faith in the midst of an alien culture or ideology? Alexander had
imprinted on the world the significant and vibrant culture of Hellenism, characterized by a particular style of architecture, art, literature and philosophy. Other cultures were easily dominated by or
assimilated into Hellenism. Among the Jewish people some longed
for assimilation with Hellenism and sought to take the best of Greek
thought and wed it to Hebrew religious thought. Other Jews were

The Empire of Alexander

fiercely opposed to any process of inculturation and stressed the importance of distance from Hellenism and Hebrew separateness. At this time the large community of Greek-speaking Jews in Alexandria translated the Hebrew Bible into Greek. Because it was believed that the work of translation had been accomplished by seventy elders, this version came to be called the "Septuagint." The literary and philosophical sources available to Jewish scholars in the great library of Alexandria tended to open the Jews in the diaspora to the influences of Hellenism, whereas Jews in Judah, in their less sophisticated and more rustic environment, showed great hostility to Greek ideas.

When Antiochus Epiphanes sought to impose Hellenism on the territory of Palestine a prominent Jewish family, the Maccabees, rose up to oppose his efforts. Around 166 B.C.E. Mattathias and his five sons began to attack the political might of Antiochus.

Then the king's officers spoke to Mattathias as follows: "You are a leader, honored and great in this city, and supported by sons and brothers. Now be the first to come and do what the king commands, as all the Gentiles and the men of Judah and those that are left in Jerusalem have done. Then you and your sons will be numbered among the friends of the king. . . ."

But Mattathias answered and said in a loud voice: "Even if all the nations that live under the rule of the king obey him and have chosen to do his commandments, departing each one from the religion of his fathers, yet I and my sons and my brothers will live by the covenant of our fathers. . . . We will not obey the king's words by turning aside from our religion. . . ."

A Jew came forward in the sight of all to offer sacrifice upon the altar in Modein, according to the king's command. When Mattathias saw it, he burned with zeal and his heart was stirred. He gave vent to righteous anger; he ran and killed him upon the altar . . . and he and his sons fled to the hills and left all they had in the city.

Then many who were seeking righteousness and justice went down to the wilderness to dwell there . . . and all who became fugitives to escape their troubles joined them (Mattathias and his sons) and reinforced them. They organized an army and struck down sinners in their anger and lawless men in their wrath; the survivors fled to the Gentiles for safety. And Mattathias and his friends went about and tore down the altars; they forceably circumcised all the uncircumcised boys that they found within the bor-

ders of Israel. . . . They rescued the law out of the hands of the
Gentiles and kings, and they never let the sinner gain the upper
hand (1 Macc 2:17–48).

Finally one son, Judas, succeeded in defeating the Seleucid army.
In 165 B.C.E. Judas rededicated the temple of Jerusalem. This event
is remembered yearly by the Jewish people through the December
festival of lights, Hanukkah. The Maccabean guerrilla movement
had triumphed and Israel once again knew a kind of independence.

However, a new power, Rome, emerged in the Mediterranean
basin. In 63 B.C.E. the Roman general, Pompey, conquered Jerusalem. The Romans ruled Palestine for over one hundred years. At
times they set up puppet kings and high priests to do their work for
them. In 37 B.C.E. they named Herod the Great as ruler; it was he
who rebuilt the temple of Jerusalem on a magnificent scale. After
the death of Herod in 4 B.C.E. Rome chose to rule through a system
of procurators.

4

The Ancient Religions and the God of Israel

The Meaning of Religion

Religion is an abiding human phenomenon which is difficult to define because it can be approached from so many different perspectives. The phenomenon of religion can be and must be looked at philosophically, theologically, sociologically, historically, and comparatively. Obviously, the best way to understand religion would be to use all of these different approaches since religion has to do with the whole of human existence. Religion touches the whole person in the totality of the person's relationship not only with God but also with all other persons and with the whole cosmic order as well. This is the perspective used by Richard McBrien who defines religion as:

> The whole complexus of attitudes, convictions, emotions, gestures, rituals, beliefs, and institutions by which we come to terms with, and express, our most fundamental relationship with Reality (God and the created order, perceived as coming forth from God's creative hand). That relationship is disclosed by a process we have called revelation. Religion, therefore, is our (more or less) structured response to revelation (*Catholicism*, Winston Press, 1981, p. 250).

Two prominent scholars of the twentieth century, Emile Durkheim (1858–1917) and Rudolph Otto (1869–1937), have examined in depth the basic characteristics of religion. The sociologist, Emile Durkheim, saw the sacred as some kind of force or power which is invisible, supportive and demanding. Religion is the sense of the holy or sacred elicited in the human person when he or she encounters this force or power. This awareness of the holy inspires an attitude of awe and reverence, which is a characteristic of religion.

Rudolph Otto speaks of the "mystery" of religion which simultaneously overwhelms and fascinates human beings. The experience of the mystery of the numinous or holy, as something totally other, creates feelings of unworthiness and awe in the believer.

Characteristics of Religion

Using the insights of McBrien, Durkheim and Otto as a basis, one could say that religion has the following five general characteristics:

1. Religion has been a universal phenomenon found in almost all cultures throughout time.
2. Religion necessarily involves faith which is a personal knowledge of God. The content of that faith may differ from religion to religion, and even within the same religion there will be differences of interpretation. Religion itself necessitates some awareness of the holy, the sacred, the ultimate or God.
3. Religion, as a response to the holy, expresses itself in a system of religious beliefs which are articulated in a creed or a set of doctrines.
4. Religion also expresses itself outwardly in various forms of human activity. Ritual, worship or liturgy expresses the human response to the holy in a public fashion. Moral behavior or ethical conduct carries out in daily life the core beliefs that a person accepts. Ethical conduct represents, in the public and private forum, one's commitment to the values resulting from the faith that flows from the encounter with the holy.
5. Religion generates a community of shared perceptions, meanings and values. Community of its very nature requires structure and organization. Structure and organization call for a division of labor, and so different functions develop for different persons within the religious community.

Religions of the Ancient World

Mesopotamian Religion

The civilization that thrived between the Tigris and Euphrates Rivers, three thousand years before the birth of Christ, believed in a pantheon of gods. While all the gods had to be appeased, each Mesopotamian city-state believed itself to be the prize of a particular god. Because the life experience of the Mesopotamian people was one of insecurity, victimization and dependence on whimsical natural forces, the general feeling of the people toward the gods was fearful. The unpredictable flooding of the two great rivers, the Tigris and Euphrates, was seen as a punishment by the gods, who had to be appeased by worship and catered to by offering sacrifice. Thus the gods were perceived as jealous and petty deities who were rather indifferent to human beings and their plight. The gods, however, demanded honor and respect in worship. This was rendered to them in the terraced temples, the ziggurats, which served as their symbolic houses located at the center of every Mesopotamian city.

Egyptian Religion

Ancient Egyptian civilization, except for a brief period during the new kingdom (1570–1085 B.C.E.), was polytheistic. The exception was the reign of Amenhotep IV (1379–1362 B.C.E.) who changed his name to Akhnaton and introduced the worship of the sun as the single divine force in the universe. As was true in Mesopotamia, different cities worshiped different gods, and particular gods played more prominent roles in specific localities.

In contrast to the Mesopotamian view of the gods, the Egyptian understanding saw the gods as more benevolent and caring. This belief was related to the more stable character of Egyptian political and social life and the orderly and predictable way in which the Nile River flooded annually.

The pharaoh was the representative of the gods among the people and shared in their divinity as a god in his own right. As such the pharaoh and his policies were seen as manifestations of the divine will for the order of the universe. Hence the wishes of the pharaoh were to be accepted and obeyed without question.

The Egyptians had a deep belief in an afterlife which was the continuation and perfection of life here on earth. The pyramids of Corfu and the tombs in the Valley of the Kings, near Luxor, are the enduring architectural witnesses of this important feature of Egyptian religion.

The priests of the various gods such as Amon-Re and Osiris occupied a very important place in Egyptian society as a whole as well as within Egyptian religion in particular. At times in the history of Egypt the priests of the various gods achieved great political power and amassed considerable wealth, thus posing a threat to any pharaoh who did not accommodate himself to their way of thinking.

Greek Religion

The gods of classical Greece were divinized projections of the Greek ideals of beauty, wisdom, and power. The deities of Greece manifested all the complexity of the human patterns of behavior, emotions and attitudes, sometimes being petty and vindictive and at other times benevolent and caring.

Apollo

Before 800 B.C.E. the chief gods were nature gods to whom human sacrifice was offered at times to insure divine assistance in maintaining the fertility of the rocky soil of Greece. In an agrarian culture, whose very existence depended on wheat, wine and olive oil, obtaining the blessing of the gods became an absolute necessity worth any sacrifice. Due to the immense impact of the Homeric epics of the Iliad and the Odyssey, after 800 B.C.E., the gods of Greece were anthropomorphized and came to live on Mount Olympus. The gods who inhabited Olympus were perfect in body, strong, ageless, and immortal. They made no ethical demands upon individuals or the city-states of Greece. But because they were superior beings and could be offended, it was necessary to gain their favor and retain their good will. The sacrificial rites offered by the priests in the temples served not only to placate the gods but as fellowship meals which bound the worshipers together in a common experience of human and religious community.

Within the Greek pantheon, Zeus is the father of the gods and the supreme deity who is the source of all reality. The two brothers of Zeus, who have their own spheres of influence, are Hades, lord of the underworld, and Poseidon, master of the sea who reigns from a palace in the watery depths. Two contrasting male Greek gods are Apollo and Dionysius. Apollo is the god of wisdom who has the power of healing and he is also the source of justice, law and order. Dionysius, on the other hand, is the god of revelry who inspires wild enthusiasm and brings to the fore all the irrational and ecstatic aspects of human experience. Among the female deities, Athena, goddess of wisdom, and Aphrodite, goddess of beauty, occupied a prominent place in the religious life of the Greeks.

Unlike the Egyptians, the Greeks did not have a positive understanding of the afterlife. Death led neither to a place of reward nor to a place of punishment, but simply to the dark and minimal way of existence that was Hades.

In the early history of Greece, the gods offered explanations for many of the puzzling questions that one encounters during life. The activities of the gods explain both the events of nature that are beyond human control and the complex patterns of happenings which mark life in society.

The emergence of philosophy within the development of Greek civilization meant that reason rather than mythology was used to explain the events of nature and human society. This is not to say that the philosophers of ancient Greece did not have a place for the divine or religion in their world-view. They indeed believed in the divine, but not as manifest in the anthropomorphic gods of Mount Olympus. Rather they preferred a more abstract description of God as the "unmoved mover" or the "uncaused cause." This Greek philosophic understanding would become profoundly important at a later stage in the development of Western civilization when Judaism and Christianity tried to interpret the monotheism of Hebrew religion for a pagan world.

Hebrew Religion and the God of Israel

The God of the Hebrews was a unique God who stood alone as the universal God of all nations. The Hebrews knew this God, who had revealed himself in the exodus experience, as one who constantly made ethical demands on his people.

Nineteenth century German biblical scholars argued that the God of the Hebrews evolved over the course of time into a single God. They suggest that the very earliest "apiru" were animists, i.e., they worshiped spirits dwelling in nature. Then they became polytheists, worshiping many gods. Later, they moved to a system of henotheism where, while there were many gods, each had his own unchallenged area or sphere of influence. Thus, the Hebrews worshiped the territorial God of Palestine, while, for example, the Babylonians worshiped the gods of Mesopotamia. A final development was that of monaltry in which there were many gods but the Hebrews worshiped the best or the strongest deity among the pantheon. While nineteenth century scholars suggested this kind of development for the Hebrew people, today others suggest an explosion theory of divine intervention and self-revelation within Hebrew history.

Hebrew religion is monotheist, which is to say that the Hebrews believed in one single God, who was understood to be a universal God, a God for all people and not only the God of Israel. The Book of Genesis portrays God as creating all of the world and not just some portion of it. The God of the Hebrews is seen as an ethical God who makes demands on his people. At Mount Sinai God enters into a covenant wherein he promises to be faithful to his chosen or elected people, and they in turn are expected to obey his law or Torah. The law dictated the lifestyle of the people and reflected how a human person was to relate to God, to others, to self and to material things.

The Ten Commandments

"I, the LORD, am your God, who brought you out of the land of Egypt, that place of slavery. You shall not have other gods besides me. You shall not carve idols for yourselves in the shape of anything in the sky above or on the earth below or in the waters beneath the earth; you shall not bow down before them or worship them. For I, the LORD, your God, am a jealous God, inflicting punishment for their fathers' wickedness on the children of those who hate me, down to the third and fourth generation; but bestowing mercy down to the thousandth generation, on the children of those who love me and keep my commandments.

"You shall not take the name of the LORD, your God, in vain. For the LORD will not leave unpunished him who takes his name in vain.

"Remember to keep holy the sabbath day. Six days you may labor and do all your work, but the seventh day is the sabbath of the LORD, your God. No work may be done then either by you, or your son or daughter, or your male or female slave, or your beast, or by the alien who lives with you. In six days the LORD made the heavens and the earth, the sea and all that is in them; but on the seventh day he rested. That is why the LORD has blessed the sabbath day and made it holy.

"Honor your father and your mother, that you may have a long life in the land which the LORD, your God, is giving you.

"You shall not kill.

"You shall not commit adultery.

"You shall not steal.

"You shall not bear false witness against your neighbor.

"You shall not covet your neighbor's wife, nor his male or female slave, nor his ox or ass, nor anything else that belongs to him."

The Hebrew God was seen to be transcendent, totally other and spiritual; thus Hebrew religion rejected anthropomorphism. At the same time, the all-holy and resplendent God was also immanently acting within history. God was caring, loving and provident, ruling according to a plan. God was both just, punishing wrongdoing when it occurred, and also merciful, forgiving the sins of the people when they repented of their wrongdoing. The Hebrew Bible reflects this tension between God's justice and mercy, as well as the tension between God's goodness and power and the presence of evil in the world.

The Hebrew people lived according to the Torah, which was the written law that God had given to Moses—the decalogue or ten commandments. Over the years commentaries and interpretations were written on the basic law; this collection was called the Mishna. The process continued and so commentaries and interpretations were written on the Mishna as well as the Torah. The whole collection of commentaries and interpretations of the Torah and the Mishna is known as the Talmud. Life according to the Talmud gives the Jewish people their identity and differentiates them from other people.

Before the period of the monarchy, the Jewish people worshiped at various shrines. Under Solomon and his successors, worship and ritual was centered in the temple of Jerusalem. During the exile, when the temple in Jerusalem had been destroyed, worship took place in small gathering places, the synagogues. The temple was rebuilt after the return from exile, but the synagogues of the exilic period continued in a new setting as an essential feature of Jewish worship. While animal sacrifices as well as cereal offerings were the chief ritual acts in the temple, worship in the synagogues centered on the study of the Torah, the word of God.

The priests of the shrines in the early days and later at the temple in Jerusalem were religious officials whose main concern was the offering of various kinds of sacrifice. During the exile teaching priests, who at a later date would come to be called rabbis, emerged as religious leaders when temple worship was no longer possible. The main concern of the teaching priests was not sacrifice but the study and explanation of the Torah. With the return from the exile, the sacrificial priesthood and the teaching priesthood came to exist side by side as distinct but interrelated aspects of the Jewish worship tradition.

The Hebrew religion went through various stages of development, emphasizing at different times different expectations. During the exile a people longing for freedom began to focus anew upon the covenant and the promise of God. The center of this new vision of themselves as a covenant people, living by the promises of God, was the coming of the Messiah. They believed that he would set the people free and lead them back to their own land and their identity as a holy nation, an alternative community.

FOR FURTHER READING

Lawrence Boadt, *Reading the Old Testament* (Mahwah, New Jersey: Paulist Press, 1984).

Walter Brueggemann, *The Prophetic Imagination* (Philadelphia: Fortress Press, 1980). This is a fine book which influenced our treatment of prophecy. We have used the "call to be an alternative community" as descriptive of not only Moses' call but as the call or mission of the great prophets of Israel, Jesus, the apostles and the entire Church community.

Abba Eban, *Heritage: Civilization and the Jews* (New York: Summit Books, 1984). This is the companion volume to the acclaimed television series of the same name.

Leo Trepp, *A History of the Jewish Experience* (New York, N.Y.: Behrman House, Inc., 1973).

5

Judaism Within the Greco-Roman World

The Empires of Alexander the Great and Rome

When Alexander the Great conquered Jerusalem in 332 B.C.E., the Jews of Palestine were confronted with the art, architecture, literature and philosophy of Greek culture, which served as the bonding elements for this new world empire. Hellenistic culture was the fusion of Greek culture, Hellenism, with ideas, values and social structures present among the various conquered peoples. Prior to Alexander the Great some Jews had been living in the Persian Empire. The Jews of Palestine as well as the Jews of the diaspora had to decide how to relate to the Hellenistic culture which formed the matrix of Alexander's empire.

Many Jews reacted negatively to this culture, retreating into isolation; others, however, welcomed elements of Hellenistic culture and rejoiced in them. The question for the Jews, of course, was always the question of faith and culture. How could they maintain a pure form of Hebrew faith in the face of the challenges provided by either a local culture or the culture of an entire empire? The response was always the same. Some refused to inculturate and lived as a sect alongside the dominant culture. Other Jews however, Jews of the diaspora, living in such centers of the empire as Alexandria in Egypt, Antioch in Syria and cities in Greece itself, sought to somehow wed the best elements of culture with Hebrew faith.

After the death of Alexander his generals divided up the empire. Palestine was first under the control of the Ptolemies of Egypt and then passed to the control of the Seleucid dynasty of Syria. The latter, in particular, insisted on the Hellenization of Palestine and the Jewish people.

When Seleucus died and Antiochus who was called Epiphanes succeeded to the kingdom, Jason the brother of Onias obtained the high priesthood by corruption, promising the king at an interview three hundred and sixty talents of silver and, from another source of revenue, eighty talents. In addition to this he promised to pay one hundred and fifty more if permission were given to establish by his authority a gymnasium and a body of youth for it, and to enroll the men of Jerusalem as citizens of Antioch. When the king assented and Jason came to office, he at once shifted his country-men over to the Greek way of life. He set aside the existing royal concessions to the Jews, secured through John the father of Eupole-mus, who went on the mission to establish friendship and alliance with the Romans; and he destroyed the lawful ways of living and introduced new customs contrary to the law. For with alacrity he founded a gymnasium right under the citadel, and he induced the noblest of the young men to wear the Greek hat. There was such an extreme of Hellenization and increase in the adoption of foreign ways because of the surpassing wickedness of Jason, who was ungodly and no high priest, that the priests were no longer intent upon their service at the altar. Despising the sanctuary and ne-glecting the sacrifices, they hastened to take part in the unlawful proceedings in the wrestling arena after the call to the discus, disdaining the honors prized by their fathers and putting the high-est value upon Greek forms of prestige (2 Macc 4:7–15).

This attempt at Hellenization provoked a strong reaction on the part of the Jews. Judas Maccabeus and his brothers, the members of the family of Mattathias, led an armed revolt against the Seleucids, eventually gaining independence. About one hundred years later, continued unrest in the Near East finally provoked the intervention of Rome, which was emerging as the center of a new world empire.

Palestine became part of the Roman Empire after Pompey's con-quest of Jerusalem in 63 B.C.E. In 37 B.C.E. Rome permitted Herod the Great to become king of Israel, although he remained subject to strict Roman supervision. Herod ruled until 4 B.C.E. and was king at the time of the birth of Christ. Herod was a great builder who constructed many new cities such as Caesarea in Palestine and greatly refurbished the temple in Jerusalem. At Herod's death the kingdom of Israel was divided among his three sons: Herod Arche-laus was given Judah and Galilee; Herod Antipas received Samaria and Perea; Herod Philip was awarded the northern provinces. Because there was great discontent under the three sons of Herod, all were eventually replaced by an official of the empire, the procurator.

Palestine became a conquered nation once again, dominated by the power of Rome which insisted on a system of taxation. The Jews greatly resented this taxation because for them God alone should receive tribute and taxes. Roman domination was not only political and economic exploitation but also religious control. While the Jews were permitted to observe their religion, the high priesthood was often in the hands of the leading political families who were, in effect, puppets of Rome.

Thus Roman officials and the Roman army controlled the political, social, religious and economic life of Palestine, maintaining a regime of injustice and oppression which led to a growing opposition and unrest within the Jewish population. The resentment of the Palestinian Jews against their Roman oppressors finally led to the Jewish uprising of 66–73 C.E. All the military might of Rome moved into Palestine to quell this insurrection, destroying the temple and a considerable part of the city of Jerusalem in 70 C.E. Nevertheless the Jewish people, amid terrible physical and psychological suffering, continued to hold out against the might of Rome. About one thousand Jewish soldiers retreated to the garrison of Masada where they made a heroic final stand against the might of Rome. When, in 73 C.E., the Roman conquest of their last stronghold seemed inevitable, the valiant defenders of Masada, in a symbolic rejection of the power of this world, committed suicide rather than surrender to the Romans.

The Jewish World of Palestine

The Sadducees

Among the numerous disparate Jewish parties or factions in Palestine at the time of Jesus of Nazareth, one of the main religio-political groups was the party of the Sadducees. This Jewish group of aristocrats and establishmentarians had been organized around 200 B.C.E. and were allied both with the high priests of the temple and

63 Romans conquer Judea	37 Herod named king of Jews	BCE	CE
			c. 0 Jesus born

with the Roman rulers of Palestine. While many of the Sadducees had adopted the prevalent culture—the Hellenistic culture of the Greco-Roman world—they were also religious conservatives. Thus they accepted only written law or Torah and rejected all interpretations of that law. They were the party of the privileged who supported the status quo and did not advocate independence from Rome because that might threaten their power and influence. Still, they were truly a Jewish party.

The Pharisees

The Pharisees were another group or faction among the Jews at the time of Jesus. They became a force after the era of Judas Maccabeus and the rededication of the temple. The Pharisees were more liberal than the Sadducees in religious matters, especially in interpreting the law or Torah which they saw as constantly evolving. The Pharisees encouraged religious worship in the home and synagogue as well as supporting the rights of the temple. While the Pharisees saw Roman domination as a divine punishment for Israel's unfaithfulness they did not advocate armed rebellion against Rome as a solution to this domination. Rather they looked to the coming of a deliverer, a messiah, and sought to prepare for his coming by reforming their lives and renewing Judaism through a rededication to the covenant as the center of Jewish life. The commitment of the Pharisees to the ongoing evolution of Jewish life and thought made them strong advocates of education encouraging all to study the law or Torah as a basis for their lives.

The Zealots

A third party, the Zealots, insisted that no Jew living in Palestine had any business paying tribute to Rome or acknowledging any rights of the Roman emperor over the Jewish people. The Zealots were prepared to wage war against Rome and were, in a sense, guerrilla warriors who had banded together in an underground movement for the sake of Jewish independence. For sixty years they harassed Rome with occasional warfare until finally they succeeded

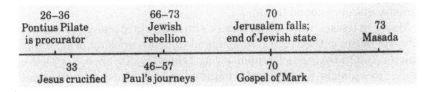

26–36	66–73	70	
Pontius Pilate	Jewish	Jerusalem falls;	73
is procurator	rebellion	end of Jewish state	Masada
33	46–57	70	
Jesus crucified	Paul's journeys	Gospel of Mark	

in provoking the war between Rome and the Jews in Palestine which ended in 73 C.E. The revolt led to the slaughter of thousands of Jews and the physical destruction of Jerusalem and many other Jewish centers in Palestine.

The Essenes

The Essenes were something of an elitist group who lived an ascetic and celibate life in desert communes. They saw only corruption in the world around them, both inside and outside of Judaism. Thus they rejected Rome as well as the Judaism of the high priesthood of the temple. While they awaited the coming of a great liberator who would set Israel free, their concern, as sons of light, was to maintain ritual purity and engage in unremitting study of Torah.

Jewish Society in Palestine

While the Roman procurator had absolute authority in Palestine, the Jewish people were allowed to have some self-determination as a nation through the Sanhedrin. This senate of seventy members presided over by the high priests and dominated by the priestly and aristocratic families exercised authority within limited areas of Jewish life, e.g., they could try to condemn someone to death for a serious crime but could not carry out the death penalty without the approval of the Roman procurator.

The upper and middle classes often chose to belong to one of the parties described above. However, the majority of Jews did not belong to any of these parties. They were, in a sense, the outcasts of society: the poor, the sick and "sinful."

The poor included beggars and the sick, the disabled—the blind, deaf, mute, etc.—as well as widows and orphans, unskilled laborers, peasants and slaves. They were, in effect, those who were almost totally dependent on others for subsistence.

The sick were another category of people in Israel at the time of Jesus. Since illness very often accompanied poverty and was caused by it, there were a great many sick people in Palestine whose illnesses were both physical and psychic. The sick were often outcasts because their illnesses were thought to be the result of God's punishment occasioned by sin.

Many in Israel were considered "sinners" and thus were social outcasts because their work was judged to be an unclean profession which vitiated their Jewish identity as defined by Torah, e.g., prostitutes, tax collectors, shepherds, money lenders. Those who did not pay taxes to the priests or who neglected the sabbath and ritual purifications were also reckoned as sinners. Since Jewish identity came from observance of the law or Torah, one had to be able first to read the law so one could know it and observe it. The illiterate were reckoned among the sinners because they constantly broke the precepts of the law which they could not read and thus not know and hence not observe.

The Jewish World of the Diaspora

The Jews of the diaspora or the Jews who lived outside of Palestine throughout the Roman empire and in the Parthian empire to the east, where many Jews had chosen to stay after the exile, far outnumbered their brothers and sisters in the land of promise—*eretz Israel*. The exact number of the Jews living in the diaspora is unknown but we do know that there were a million Jews living in Egypt with their center in Alexandria in the first century of the Christian era. At that time there were also eleven or twelve synagogues in Rome. These two facts tell us several important things about the Jews of the diaspora. First, for the most part their language was either Greek or Latin in contrast to the Palestinian Jews who spoke Aramaic. Second, because they were at a great geographical distance from Palestine, the center of their community life and worship was the local synagogue rather than the temple of Jerusalem.

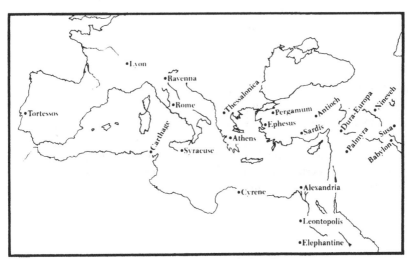

Jewish Communities of the Diaspora

Confronted as they were on all sides with both the positive and negative aspects of Hellenistic culture, the Jews had to struggle with preserving the essentials of the Jewish faith while making necessary adaptations to the necessities of daily life in an environment that was often hostile. The translation of the Hebrew Bible into Greek at Alexandria in the third century B.C.E., the Septuagint, and the subsequent "wisdom" literature written by Jewish rabbis in the same cultural milieu testify both to the learning of the diaspora communities and their missionary zeal. The great Alexandrian Jewish thinker, Philo (20 B.C.E.–50 C.E.) sought to harmonize Hebrew thought and Platonic philosophy as a bridge between Jewish culture and Hellenistic culture. The Book of Wisdom, written in Alexandria by a diaspora Jew, exemplifies the attempt of both the Jews and the Greeks to find meaning within the Hellenistic culture which prized wisdom as a central life value.

May God grant that I speak with judgment and have thoughts worthy of what I have received, for he is the guide even of wisdom and the corrector of the wise. For both we and our words are in his hand, as are all understanding and skill in crafts. For it is he who gave me unerring knowledge of what exists, to know the structure of the world and the activity of the elements; the beginning and end and middle of times, the alternations of the solstices and the changes of the seasons, the cycles of the year and the constellations of the stars, the natures of animals and the tempers of wild beasts, the powers of spirits and the reasonings of men, the varieties of plants and the virtues of roots; I learned both what is secret and what is manifest, for wisdom, the fashioner of all things, taught me (Wis 7:15–22).

Jesus of Nazareth would be born within the world of Palestinian Judaism between 8 and 4 B.C.E., and after his death and resurrection his disciples would take the message of his life and teachings, the Gospel, to the world of Hellenistic culture, beginning always as St. Paul did within the synagogues of the diaspora. Jewish life and culture remain an integral part of the Western experience since the central religious truths and moral values of the West are the inheritance from the Jewish people.

6

The Sources and Content of the Life and Teaching of Jesus

The New Testament as Revealed Word

The New Testament is a collection of twenty-seven books written over the course of approximately seventy-five years by different authors for different early Christian communities. The authors of the books of the New Testament had diverse purposes in mind and used a variety of literary forms to recount the deeds and teachings of Jesus or about Jesus. Christians believe that these writings are "inspired," meaning that they were composed with the assistance of the grace of the Holy Spirit acting as a guiding principle, moving the human author to write what God wanted and the way God wanted. From the perspective of the Christian faith, the words of the New Testament are the revealed word of God and at the same time remain human words since they are the product of the human, socially-conditioned author. Thus both the Christian Scriptures, as also the Hebrew Scriptures, are believed to be the revealed word of God, God's verbal self-disclosure, which manifests the divine plan of salvation.

The Content of the New Testament

The New Testament is a collection of books which are, in fact, different types of literature, e.g., Gospels, the Acts of the Apostles, which is a theological history of the early Church, letters of various apostles and a visionary account of the end of time and the heavenly kingdom, the Book of Revelation or the Apocalypse. Written in Koine or common Greek, the books of the New Testament were written over a period of seventy-five years (see box).

The Composition of the New Testament

50–60	Paul the Apostle	
	1 Thessalonians	*Philippians*
	Galatians	*Romans*
	1, 2 Corinthians	*Philemon*
70–90	Paul's Disciples	
	2 Thessalonians	
	Colossians	
	Ephesians	
70–80	*Gospel of Mark*	
	Gospel of	
	Matthew	
c. 85	*Gospel of Luke*	
	Acts of the	
	Apostles	
85–90	*Hebrews*	
c. 90	*Gospel of John*	
	1, 2, 3 John	
	Revelation	
100–140	*James*	
	1, 2 Peter	
	Jude	
c. 125	*1, 2 Timothy*	
	Titus	

Between 50 and 60 C.E. the apostle Paul wrote letters to various Christian communities: 1 Thessalonians, Galatians, 1 and 2 Corinthians, Philippians, Romans and a letter to his convert Philemon. Later between the years 70 and 90 the disciples of Paul wrote 2 Thessalonians, Colossians and Ephesians. During the last decades of the first century of the Christian era, unknown Christian authors wrote the Gospels according to Matthew and Mark and a two volume work, the Gospel of Luke and the Acts of the Apostles. The three letters and the Gospel ascribed to John were composed between 80 and 100. The Book of Revelation, produced by a Church leader exiled to the island of Patmos between 90 and 100, also comes down to us under the name of the apostle John. During the final period of New Testament composition, unknown early Christian writers produced 1 and 2 Peter, the Letters of James and Jude, 1 and 2 Timothy, Titus, and the Letter to the Hebrews.

The books of the New Testament, as documents of faith produced by the early Christians, are both proclamation and encouragement. They proclaim the life, death and resurrection of Jesus as well as his teachings to be true and of vital significance for human existence. At the same time these documents are encouragement, i.e., they give advice on how to live according to the teachings of Jesus by offering practical guidance for Christian behavior.

The Gospels as Literary Sources

The Gospels are a unique literary form which present the life and teaching of Jesus. The word "Gospel" means "good news," and the New Testament Gospels are understood by Christians as the good news about Jesus Christ, the bearer of human salvation. The written Gospels contained in the New Testament are the end product of a long process of the transmission of various traditions related to the deeds and sayings of Jesus. The actions of Jesus himself, e.g., his healings, journeys, ministry, passion, death and resurrection as experienced by his first disciples constitute the first level of Gospel transmission. The teachings of Jesus about the kingdom of God also belong to the first level. On the second level we find the original preaching of the disciples about Jesus' life and teaching. Finally on the third level of Gospel transmission, the oral preaching of the disciples was committed to writing. The Gospels, therefore, are written documents that flow from oral traditions about the person and actions of Jesus Christ. The Gospels are not biographies of Jesus but rather proclamations or testimonies of faith by inspired believers. They offer witness to the faith of the earliest Christian communities and are designed to convince others to believe.

Scholars suggest that the Gospel of Mark was the original written document. The unknown author of this Gospel drew upon an oral tradition that he had received as well as upon some written collection of the sayings of Jesus. The author of Matthew's Gospel used Mark's Gospel as one of his sources as well as the Q document, i.e., a collection of the sayings of Jesus and material taken from the tradition of his own Christian community. The author of Luke similarly used Mark's Gospel, the Q document and his own community tradition.

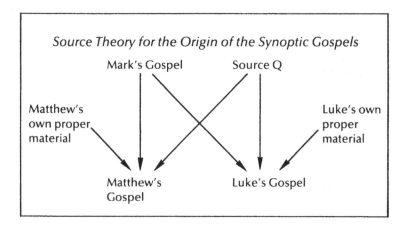

The Gospels of Matthew, Mark and Luke are called the Synoptic Gospels because when they are placed next to each other in columns there are many similarities among the three. Since there are also differences in the Synoptic Gospels, the theory of multiple sources described above accounts for the basic similarities while making room for the real differences. The obviously different character of the Gospel of John is the result of the unique traditions of the Johannine community used by the author of the fourth Gospel.

The Life of Jesus

While the Gospels of Mark and John say nothing about the birth of Jesus, the Gospels of Matthew and Luke provide some information concerning that event and its circumstances from the perspective of faith. From the latter two Gospels we learn that Mary, the mother of Jesus, gave birth to her son in Bethlehem where she and Joseph, the foster-father of Jesus, had journeyed because of a Roman census.

> In those days a decree went out from Caesar Augustus that all the world should be enrolled. This was the first enrollment, when Quirinius was governor of Syria. And all went to be enrolled, each to his own city. And Joseph also went up from Galilee, from the city of Nazareth, to Judea, to the city of David, which is called

Bethlehem, because he was of the house and lineage of David, to be enrolled with Mary, his betrothed, who was with child. And while they were there, the time came for her to be delivered. And she gave birth to her first-born son and wrapped him in swaddling cloths, and laid him in a manger, because there was no place for them in the inn (Lk 2:1–7).

Except for the story of the twelve year old Jesus being separated from his parents for three days, while he was engaged in discussing the Torah with the rabbis in the temple at Jerusalem, the Gospels say nothing about the early years of Jesus. The Gospel of Luke offers the following terse summary of that incident and Jesus' subsequent years before the beginning of his public ministry when he was about thirty years of age.

And he went down with them and came to Nazareth, and was obedient to them; and his mother kept all these things in her heart. And Jesus increased in wisdom and in stature, and in favor with God and man (Lk 2:51–52).

The Gospels use a variety of images to describe the ministry of Jesus. He is pictured as a preacher and teacher, a wandering rabbi, who calls men and women to share anew in the covenant of love between God and themselves as people of the promise. Jesus is seen as a prophet who announces the coming of God's kingdom and the passing away of the present order of things. He is the healer who restores physical and mental health to the sick and even raises the dead to life. Jesus is also the Son of God and divine reconciler who forgives sins and sets people free from their bondage to the power of evil.

That evening, at sundown, they brought to him all who were sick or possessed with demons. And the whole city was gathered together about the door. And he healed many who were sick with various diseases, and cast out many demons; and he would not permit the demons to speak, because they knew him. And in the morning, a great while before day he rose and went out to a lonely place, and there he prayed. And Simon and those who were with him pursued him, and they found him and said to him, "Every one is searching for you." And he said: "Let us go on to the next towns, that I may preach there also; for that is why I came out." And he

A woman touches the cloak of Jesus: detail from a 4th century sarcophagus.

went throughout all Galilee, preaching in their synagogues and casting out demons (Mk 1:32–39).

The central event of all the Gospels is the passion and death of Jesus. For both religious and political motives, the Jewish authorities condemned Jesus to death and handed him over to the Roman procurator, Pontius Pilate, to be crucified.

One of the criminals who were hanged railed at him, saying, "Are you not the Christ? Save yourself and us!" But the other rebuked him, saying, "Do you not fear God, since you are under the same sentence of condemnation? And we indeed justly; for we are receiving the due reward of our deeds; but this man has done nothing wrong." And he said, "Jesus, remember me when you come into your kingdom." And he said to him, "Truly, I say to you, today you will be with me in Paradise." It was now about the sixth hour, and there was darkness over the whole land until the ninth hour, while the sun's light failed; and the curtain of the temple was torn in two. Then Jesus, crying with a loud voice, said, "Father, into thy hands I commit my spirit!" And having said this he breathed his last. Now when the centurion saw what had taken place, he praised God, and said, "Certainly this man was innocent!" And all the multitudes who assembled to see the sight, when they saw what had taken place, returned home beating their breasts. And all his acquaintances and the women who had followed him from Galilee stood at a distance and saw these things (Lk 23:39–49).

Christians believe that Jesus was raised from the dead a few days later, and that in his risen body he appeared to his followers before being taken up into heaven, telling them to continue his mission of preaching, teaching, healing and reconciling.

Now after the sabbath, toward the dawn of the first day of the week, Mary Magdalene and the other Mary went to the sepulchre. And behold, there was a great earthquake; for an angel of the Lord descended from heaven and came and rolled back the stone, and sat upon it. His appearance was like lightning, and his raiment white as snow. And for fear of him the guards trembled and became like dead men. But the angel said to the women, "Do not be afraid; for I know that you seek Jesus who was crucified. He is not here; for he has risen, as he said. Come, see the place where he lay. Then go quickly and tell his disciples that he has risen from the dead, and behold, he is going before you to Galilee; there you will see him. Lo, I have told you." So they departed quickly from the tomb with fear and great joy, and ran to tell his disciples. And behold, Jesus met them and said, "Hail!" And they came up and took hold of his feet and worshiped him. Then Jesus said to them, "Do not be afraid; go and tell my brethren to go to Galilee, and there they will see me." . . . Now the eleven disciples went to Galilee, to the mountain to which Jesus had directed them. And when they saw him they worshiped him; but some doubted. And Jesus came and said to them, "All authority in heaven and on earth has been given to me. Go therefore and make disciples of all nations, baptizing them in the name of the Father, and of the Son, and of the Holy Spirit, teaching them to observe all that I have commanded you; and lo, I am with you always, to the close of the age" (Mt 28:1–10, 16–20).

The basic framework for the story of Jesus is rather simple—birth, ministry, passion, death and resurrection. Although the early Christians knew very little about the life of Jesus, they felt that what the Gospels contained was sufficient.

Now Jesus did many other signs in the presence of the disciples, which are not written in this book; but these are written that you may believe that Jesus is the Christ, the Son of God, and that believing you may have life in his name (Jn 20:30–31).

The Teachings of Jesus

The Kingdom of God as Alternative Community

The primary focus for the teaching of Jesus of Nazareth was the kingdom of God. Jesus himself and subsequently his disciples interpreted his prophetic mission as the proclamation and definitive inauguration of the kingdom of God. The biblical metaphor "kingdom of God" or "reign of God" does not refer to a geographical place or to a specific political, social or economic system. Rather it means the active presence of God in human history, caring, loving and supporting the lives of individuals and the community life of the people with whom he has made a covenant. Jesus saw his mission as announcing and making present this vision of God's relatedness to human beings in and through his preaching, healing, reconciling and finally his death.

The kingdom of God, as proclaimed by Jesus, was an alternative way of understanding who God is, what it meant to be human and what it meant to belong to a community. It offered an alternative pattern for human life that stood in marked contrast both to the values of the Hellenistic culture of the Roman empire and to the sectarian and restrictive outlook that characterized many groups within Palestinian Judaism. The kingdom of God preached by Jesus was to be the way of life of a new people whose guiding principle would be love of God and love of neighbor. The style of life for this alternative community was to be the service of others in pursuit of mercy, justice and peace. Although they knew that the ideals of the kingdom could never be fully realized within history, the early followers of Jesus still believed that by God's grace they could truly begin to live in the kingdom now while waiting for its fullness in the world to come.

Jesus experienced God as a loving Father who called human beings his sons and daughters and invited them to share in the divine pattern of love by being brothers and sisters to one another. The Holy Spirit, who was the gift of the compassionate Father through the death and resurrection of his beloved Son Jesus to the community of believers, was understood to be the source of power who made possible this alternative way of relating to others.

But love your enemies, and do good, and lend, expecting nothing in return; and your reward will be great, and you will be sons of the Most High; for he is kind to the ungrateful and the selfish. Be merciful, even as your Father is merciful. Judge not, and you will not be judged; condemn not, and you will not be condemned; forgive, and you will be forgiven; give, and it will be given to you; good measure, pressed down, shaken together, running over, will be put into your lap. For the measure you give will be the measure you get back (Lk 6:35–38).

If you ask anything in my name, I will do it. If you love me, you will keep my commandments. And I will pray to the Father, and he will give you another Counselor, to be with you for ever, even the Spirit of truth, whom the world cannot receive, because it neither sees him nor knows him; you know him, for he dwells with you, and will be in you. I will not leave you desolate; I will come to you. Yet a little while, and the world will see me no more, but you will see me; because I live, you will live also. In that day you will know that I am in my Father, and you in me, and I in you. He who has my commandments and keeps them, he it is who loves me; and he who loves me will be loved by my Father, and I will love him and manifest myself to him (Jn 14:14–21).

The Options of Jesus

One can understand Jesus and his mission by considering the options that he chose during his ministry. The initial action of Jesus was to align himself with the preaching of John the Baptist rather than joining one of the many sects within Palestinian Judaism. John's message was one of challenge and hope that called the Jewish people to conversion and an alternative style of life in accord with the prophetic understanding of mercy and justice. Although he predicted the approaching judgment of God, he also offered hope in the promised coming of the Messiah who would inaugurate the kingdom of God. Jesus' acceptance of baptism at the hands of John symbolized his own commitment to continuing and expanding the message and mission of the last and greatest of the prophets of Israel.

> Now when he heard that John had been arrested, he withdrew into Galilee. . . . From that time Jesus began to preach, saying, "Repent, for the kingdom of heaven is at hand." And he went about all Galilee, teaching in their synagogues and preaching the gospel of the kingdom and healing every disease and every infirmity among the people. So his fame spread throughout all Syria, and they brought him all the sick, those afflicted with various diseases and pains, demoniacs, epileptics, and paralytics, and he healed them. And great crowds followed him from Galilee and the Decapolis and Jerusalem and Judea and from beyond the Jordan. Seeing the crowds, he went up on the mountain, and when he sat down his disciples came to him. And he opened his mouth and taught them, saying: "Blessed are the poor in spirit, for theirs is the kingdom of heaven. Blessed are those who mourn, for they shall be comforted. Blessed are the meek, for they shall inherit the earth. Blessed are those who hunger and thirst for righteousness, for they shall be satisfied. Blessed are the merciful, for they shall obtain mercy. Blessed are the pure in heart, for they shall see God. Blessed are the peacemakers, for they shall be called sons of God. Blessed are those who are persecuted for righteousness' sake, for theirs is the kingdom of heaven. Blessed are you when men revile you and persecute you and utter all kinds of evil against you falsely on my account. Rejoice and be glad, for your reward is great in heaven, for so men persecuted the prophets who were before you (Mt 4:12, 17, 23–25; 5:1–12).

Throughout the Gospels Jesus constantly chooses to preach the alternative community of the kingdom of God by concerning himself with the poor, the sick and sinners. Jesus seeks to give new life and hope and to free from fear and oppression those who are outsiders and feel rejected by the society around them. Jesus' option is not against the upper classes or the middle class, but he does manifest special love for those who have nothing and are alone and unwanted. The Gospels see in the life and teaching of Jesus one who fulfills all the longings of Israel for the Messiah who would set them free from oppression and renew their covenant relationship with God.

Now when John heard in prison about the deeds of the Christ, he sent word by his disciples and said to him, "Are you he who is to come, or shall we look for another?" And Jesus answered them, "Go and tell John what you hear and see: the blind receive their sight and the lame walk, lepers are cleansed and the deaf hear, and the dead are raised up, and the poor have good news preached to them. And blessed is he who takes no offense at me" (Mt 11:2–6).

7

The Mission of Paul

St. Paul is one of the most significant personalities as well as one of the greatest missionaries in the history of the Christian faith. The literary sources for the life and thought of St. Paul are his own letters and what Luke says about him in the Acts of the Apostles.

The Life of Paul

Paul was a Hebrew of the tribe of Benjamin, born in the city of Tarsus, in Cilicia, which is modern Turkey. Julius Caesar had granted independence and the right of Roman citizenship to the university city of Tarsus and consequently Paul inherited Roman citizenship. Knowing Aramaic, Hebrew and Greek, the young diaspora Jew was sent to Jerusalem to study under the famous rabbi Gamaliel. The Pharisaic party of Judaism, which Paul joined, believed that the Roman domination of Palestine was a punishment for Israel's unfaithfulness and that deliverance would come only when Israel returned to a strict observance of the Mosaic law.

Paul's Pharisaic outlook caused him to view the early Jewish Christians as traitors to the Torah and the Jewish way of life. Both the Acts of the Apostles and Paul's own testimony tell us that he persecuted Christians in his early career. He felt justified in doing so because the religious beliefs and practices of the Jewish Christians seemed to threaten the very essence of traditional Judaism.

Around the year 36, while on his way to Damascus to arrest Jewish Christians, Paul had a profound experience of religious conversion.

But Saul, still breathing threats and murder against the disciples of the Lord, went to the high priest and asked him for letters to the synagogues at Damascus, so that if he found any belonging to the Way, men or women, he might bring them bound to Jerusalem.

Now as he journeyed he approached Damascus, and suddenly a light from heaven flashed about him. And he fell to the ground and heard a voice saying, "Saul, Saul, why do you persecute me?" And he said, "Who are you, Lord?" And he said, "I am Jesus, whom you are persecuting; but rise and enter the city, and you will be told what you are to do." The men who were traveling with him stood speechless, hearing the voice but seeing no one. Saul arose from the ground; and when his eyes were opened, he could see nothing; so they led him by the hand and brought him to Damascus. And for three days he was without sight, and neither ate nor drank (Acts 9:1–9).

Subsequently Paul was instructed in the Gospel and baptized as a Christian by Ananias of Damascus. After his conversion, Paul spent some time in Arabia before beginning a preaching ministry in Damascus. Persecution by his Jewish brethren caused Paul to leave Damascus after about three years. He visited the Christian community in Jerusalem before returning to his native Tarsus. His sojourn there ended around the year 44, when the apostle Barnabas convinced him to join in the work of preaching the Gospel at Antioch in Syria, one of the greatest cities of the Roman empire.

The Christian community at Antioch commissioned Paul and Barnabas to set out on a missionary journey that lasted from 46 to 49. In the course of their travels, the missionaries preached the Gospel on the island of Cyprus and in the cities of Antioch in Pisidia, Iconium, Lystra and Derbe in Asia Minor (modern Turkey) before they returned to their center at Antioch in Syria.

Paul's missionary journey had caused a large number of Gentiles or non-Jews to embrace the Christian faith. Since Christianity up to this point had been a messianic movement within Judaism, the followers of Jesus were now confronted with the very different question of the relationship between Jews and Gentiles. Should Gentiles first become Jews in order to be baptized as Christians? Around the year 49 Paul and Barnabas, recently returned from their first missionary journey, went to Jerusalem to discuss this question with the apostles and the elders gathered there. While the Pharisaic party insisted that Gentile Christians should be circumcised, the opinion of Peter prevailed and circumcision and observance of the Mosaic law, especially the dietary laws, were not required of Gentile converts.

After his return to Antioch Paul set out on his second great missionary journey, which lasted from 49 to 52. Accompanied by Silas, Paul traveled from Syria through Cilicia to Derbe and Lystra where they recruited Timothy. After further travel in Asia Minor, visiting the regions of Phrygia and Galatia, Paul crossed over into Europe and established churches at Philippi and Thessalonica in Greece. Paul's missionary preaching in Athens, where he addressed the people on the Areopagus concerning the "Unknown God," was a failure. Following a very successful preaching ministry, lasting a year and a half in the city of Corinth, Paul visited Ephesus and Jerusalem before returning to Antioch in Syria.

Leaving Antioch two years later, Paul set out on his third missionary journey which lasted until 57. Most of that three year period was spent in evangelizing the area around Ephesus on the coast of Asia Minor and in visiting the churches he had founded in Greece. Paul's plan was to transfer his missionary activity to the western part of the Roman empire, visiting Rome and then going on to Spain. Before initiating that new phase of his ministry, Paul decided to visit Jerusalem so that he could personally bring to the impoverished Jewish Christians of that city the money he had collected from his own newly founded churches.

Arriving in Jerusalem in the late spring of 58, Paul encountered violent opposition from the Jews and was imprisoned for two years (58–60). Because of his Roman citizenship Paul was able to appeal his case to Rome, and after a very difficult journey that included shipwreck, he arrived in the capital of the empire in 61. After two years of house arrest Paul was eventually set free. Nothing is known

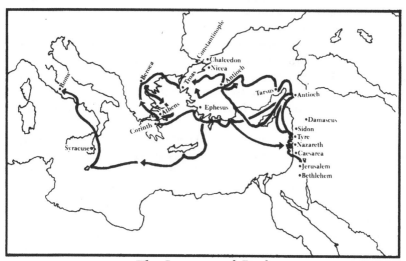

The Journeys of Paul

with certainty of the apostle's subsequent life and work. The ancient traditions of the Church, however, place his martyrdom by beheading in Rome in 67.

Between 50 and 60 Paul wrote letters or epistles to the various Christian communities that he had founded or that he hoped to visit. In the first category we find 1 Thessalonians, Galatians, 1 and 2 Corinthians, Philippians and a letter to an individual by the name of Philemon. In the second category there is a letter to the Church in Rome. The disciples of Paul wrote 2 Thessalonians, Colossians, Ephesians, 1 and 2 Timothy and Titus. Some of Paul's letters have been lost. These thirteen books of the New Testament from the hands of Paul and his disciples are the earliest works of Christian literature and the beginning of the Pauline theological tradition.

In his letters Paul, from the perspective of faith, tries to reflect upon the events of Jesus' life and his teaching so that he can understand their meaning and relevance for the life of the Christian community. Paul faced a twofold task in his work of theological reflection. First, he had to bridge the gap between the cultural and religious experience of the Jewish Christians of Palestine and that of the Jewish Christians of the diaspora as well as respond to the religious needs of Gentile converts. Second, the apostle and his disciples had to interpret the meaning of Christ by interrelating Hebraic thought forms and religious language with Greco-Roman philosophical and religious ideas and language. In Christian understanding it was finally the grace of the Holy Spirit inspiring Paul and his followers that produced the theological ideas and the masterpieces of religious literature that have nourished and renewed the Christian faith for nineteen hundred years.

Themes in Paul's Theology

Sin, Death and Justification

In Paul's view the fall or sin of Adam was a cataclysmic affair both for Adam and for all his descendants. Adam's sin radically separated him from God, and because of this sin all his descendants were also born into this state of separation. The result of this alienation was spiritual death for human beings who were cut off from God, the very source of life.

Thus men and women must be restored to God, the source of life. They must be justified. Justification for Paul was an act of reconciliation between God and the human person. Such reconciliation flowed from the merciful love of God for sinners. Justification was the beginning of God's work of salvation in each individual; that saving process reached its completion only in the fullness of the eternal life of heaven.

> Therefore sin came into the world through one man and death through sin, and so death spread to all men because all men sinned. . . . But the free gift is not like the trespass. For if many died through one man's trespass, much more have the grace of God and the free gift in the grace of that one man Jesus Christ abounded for many. . . . If, because of one man's trespass, death reigned through that one man, much more will those who receive the abundance of grace and the free gift of righteousness reign in life through the one man Jesus Christ (Rom 5:12, 15, 17).

Jesus Christ, Lord and Savior

Paul's favorite title for Jesus Christ is *Kyrios* or Lord. He used that title over one hundred and thirty-eight times in his various letters. "Lord" was a title among Greek-speaking Jews for God—one deserving of religious veneration. For Paul, Jesus, the Kyrios, was someone more than mere man and truly worthy of the highest religious veneration. Paul, of course, was writing particularly for the Gentile or Greek-speaking world and so was less concerned with Jewish titles for Jesus, such as Messiah.

Jesus was the exalted Son of God, who took on flesh and suffered and died on the cross. Christ's death on the cross was the act of reconciliation between God and sinners.

> While we were still weak, at the right time Christ died for the ungodly. Why, one will hardly die for a righteous man—though perhaps for a good man one will dare even to die. But God shows his love for us in that while we were yet sinners Christ died for us. Since, therefore, we are now justified by his blood, much more shall we be saved by him from the wrath of God. For if while we were enemies we were reconciled to God by the death of his Son,

	33 Jesus crucified		
c. 3 Paul is born	36 Conversion	44 To Antioch	46–49 First missionary journey

much more, now that we are reconciled, shall we be saved by his life. Not only so, but we also rejoice in God through our Lord Jesus Christ, through whom we have now received our reconciliation (Rom 5:6–11).

God had raised Jesus from the dead, and his resurrection was the promise that we, too, would be raised to everlasting life. Through his death and resurrection, shared by men and women in baptism, Christ made it possible for sinners to pass from death to life, from slavery to freedom.

We were buried therefore with him by baptism into death, so that as Christ was raised from the dead by the glory of the Father, we too might walk in newness of life. For if we have been united with him in a death like his, we shall certainly be united with him in a resurrection like his. We know that our old self was crucified with him so that the sinful body might be destroyed, and we might no longer be enslaved to sin. For he who has died is freed from sin. But if we have died with Christ, we believe that we shall also live with him. For we know that Christ being raised from the dead will never die again; death no longer has dominion over him. The death he died he died to sin, once for all, but the life he lives he lives to God, so you also must consider yourselves dead to sin and alive to God in Christ Jesus (Rom 6:4–11).

Law and Grace

Sin and death are a fact of human existence. The question facing each individual is how to escape or find a way out of such a condition. According to Paul the Jewish response to that question was Torah. If one lived according to Torah, especially a Pharisaic interpretation of Torah, one could find righteousness. Paul rejected the Jewish way to salvation, saying that it was no longer law but rather grace that allowed one to be saved. In this new time belief in Jesus Christ was the road to salvation. It was Christ who saved and not the law. In Galatians Paul vigorously defended the new order of things. Christ was the new Adam and it was only in and through

			66–73 Jewish revolt
49 Council of Jerusalem	49–52 Second missionary journey	54–57 Third missionary journey	67 Death in Rome

him that one could be justified. The gift of grace and faith saved one and not life in accord with the law or Torah.

> Now before faith came, we were confined under the law, kept under restraint until faith should be revealed. So the law was our custodian until Christ came, that we might be justified by faith. But now that faith has come, we are no longer under a custodian. For in Christ Jesus you are all sons of God, through faith. For as many of you as were baptized into Christ have put on Christ. There is neither Jew nor Greek, there is neither slave nor free, there is neither male nor female; for you are all one in Christ Jesus (Gal 3:23–28).

The new law for the Christian was not some external code but rather the gift of the Holy Spirit dwelling in each believer. The gift and grace of faith and the Spirit were received by the Christian in baptism. Through baptism one became an adopted child of the Father.

> But when the time had fully come, God sent forth his Son, born of woman, born under law, to redeem those who were under the law, so that we might receive adoption as sons. And because you are sons, God has sent the Spirit of his Son into our hearts, crying "Abba! Father!" So through God you are no longer a slave but a son, and if a son then an heir (Gal 4:4–7).

For Paul, Torah in past ages was necessary and a sure sign for those seeking salvation. However, Torah has been replaced by Christ and his grace. The Greek response to the question of salvation was to live according to reason or wisdom. Paul proclaimed the ultimate inadequacy of that response, for life according to reason was not possible without grace and the gift of faith. Paul's anthropology was Christ-centered and the whole cosmos was caught up in the person and saving work of Christ crucified.

> For Jews demand signs and Greeks seek wisdom, but we preach Christ crucified, a stumbling block to Jews and folly to Gentiles, but to those who are called, both Jews and Greeks, Christ the power of God and the wisdom of God. . . . He is the source of your life in Christ Jesus, whom God made our wisdom, our righteousness and sanctification and redemption; therefore, as it is written, "Let him who boasts, boast of the Lord" (1 Cor 1:22–24, 30–31).

8

The Apostolic Church—First Century Christianity

What were the original Christian communities like in their basic outlines at the dawn of Christianity? How did they differ among themselves? What did these churches have in common that made them one?

Two events in the first century of Christianity played an important role in the development of the Christian movement. The first event, which became a catalyst in shaping the future of Judaism, was the fall of Jerusalem to the Roman army in 70. After the destruction of the temple, Judaism concentrated on the Torah as authoritatively interpreted by the rabbis. They replaced the priests in the future religious direction of Judaism just as synagogues replaced the temple of Jerusalem. The destruction of the temple by the Romans sent similar shock waves throughout the Jewish Christian world. Deprived of a sacred place and of the great festival worship of the temple, Jewish Christians turned their attention even more closely to Jesus as the center of their experience of a sacred place and his life as sacred time.

The second formative event in the development of first century Christianity was the delay of the parousia. The "end-time" dominated early Christian thought, and it was believed that Jesus would return imminently as judge of the world. Some believed that the "second coming" would happen within their lifetime, that the world as they knew it would be destroyed and that a new order or creation would begin. As months and years passed, however, Christians were forced to come to terms with the delay in the parousia.

Palestinian Jewish Christianity

After the death and resurrection of Jesus his first followers came to believe and profess that he was the Messiah foretold by the prophets. They saw in Jesus the fulfillment of God's promises to send a Messiah or "anointed one" who would be both a son of David and a prophet like Moses.

For the Jewish followers of Jesus the prophet, teacher and healer from Nazareth had perfected the law of Moses and given it a new interpretation valid for all peoples. Although Jesus had been condemned for his teachings by the Jewish authorities and put to death by the Romans, the Jewish Christians believed that God had vindicated his ministry and teaching by raising him from the dead and appointing him the judge of the world to come. The first Christians, then, were a sect within Judaism itself, who were different from other Jews because they believed that Jesus was the promised Messiah. Because they were eager to fulfill the Torah as interpreted by Jesus they collected stories about Jesus and his sayings to serve as the pattern for their own lives. They also believed that the risen Jesus would teach them how to apply his teachings to their lives by sending them continually the outpouring of the Holy Spirit.

But Peter, standing with the eleven, lifted up his voice and addressed them, "Men of Judea and all who dwell in Jerusalem, let this be known to you, and give ear to my words. . . . Men of Israel, hear these words: Jesus of Nazareth, a man attested to you by God with mighty works and wonders and signs which God did through him in your midst, as you yourselves know—this Jesus, delivered up according to the definite plan and foreknowledge of God, you crucified and killed by the hands of lawless men. But God raised him up, having loosed the pangs of death, because it was not possible for him to be held by it. . . . This Jesus God raised up, and of that we all are witnesses. Being therefore exalted at the right hand of God, and having received from the Father the promise of the Holy Spirit, he has poured out this which you see and hear. . . . Let all the house of Israel therefore know assuredly that God has

		41–54 Claudius expels Jews from Rome	
c. 33 Jesus dies	c. 34 Stephen dies		66 Christians flee Jerusalem

made him both Lord and Christ, this Jesus whom you crucified" (Acts 2:14, 22–24, 32–33, 36).

The Christian Church at Jerusalem was Jewish, conservative, legalistic and conscious of its own authority. Jewish Christians continued to worship in the temple and to fulfill the law of Moses. But they also began to develop a new life-style which included a communal sharing of goods and the celebration of the Eucharist. They believed that at the Last Supper Jesus had asked his disciples to break bread together in remembrance of him as a parallel celebration to the Jewish Passover meal. This celebration of the Lord's Supper was understood as the continued renewal of God's covenant of love with his people in and through the death and resurrection of Jesus.

And they devoted themselves to the apostles' teaching and fellowship, to the breaking of bread and the prayers. And fear came upon every soul; and many wonders and signs were done through the apostles. And all who believed were together and had all things in common; and they sold their possessions and goods and distributed them to all, as any had need. And day by day, attending the temple together and breaking bread in their homes, they partook of food with glad and generous hearts, praising God and having favor with all the people. And the Lord added to their number day by day those who were being saved (Acts 2:42–47).

The Jewish Christians of Palestine lived with the hope that Jesus would soon return in glory. In the meantime they had to reform their lives in preparation for his second coming.

Repent therefore, and turn again, that your sins may be blotted out, that times of refreshing may come from the presence of the Lord, and that he may send the Christ appointed for you, Jesus, whom heaven must receive until the time for establishing all that God spoke by the mouth of his holy prophets from of old (Acts 3:19–21).

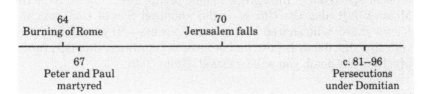

| 64 | 70 |
| Burning of Rome | Jerusalem falls |

67	c. 81–96
Peter and Paul	Persecutions
martyred	under Domitian

The destruction of the temple and the delay of the parousia forced the Jewish Christians of Palestine to rethink their relationship to Judaism and to find a new identity.

The Hellenistic Jewish-Christian Mission

Christianity was born in Palestine, but through the preaching of diaspora Jews such as the apostle Paul it quickly spread to the broader Jewish community of the Greco-Roman world. In twenty years, from 35 to 55, Christianity had moved from Palestine to the Hellenistic world, from speaking the Aramaic of Palestine to speaking the Greek of the empire ruled by Rome.

The Jews of the diaspora, who lived outside of Palestine and far from the worship of the temple, had developed their own understanding of their faith and the place of Judaism in the broader cultural mainstream of the Greco-Roman world. Palestinian Jews were suspicious of their brothers and sisters in the diaspora because they felt they had too fully accommodated themselves to Hellenistic culture and had moved away from the pure faith of Judaism.

Judaism within the diaspora, however, not only received elements of Hellenistic culture, but also influenced the surrounding environment by its strict monotheism and its demanding ethical code. Many Hellenistic Gentiles were drawn to Judaism but resisted full conversion for a variety of reasons, e.g., adult circumcision or the requisite Jewish dietary laws. These admirers of Judaism, who participated to some degree in Jewish life, came to be known as the "God-fearers."

From the beginning the Christian Church had Hellenistic or Greek speaking Jews as members. The so-called Hellenists became the spearhead of the movement of Christianity into the Hellenistic world. Because they understood that world and were missionary-minded about their faith, the Hellenists went to their brothers and sisters among the Greek speaking Jews and God-fearers and proclaimed the story of Jesus and his teaching.

Palestinian Jewish-Christians viewed Jesus in strictly Jewish categories, i.e., as the Messiah. Hellenistic Jewish-Christians used a broader spectrum of interpretation, believing Jesus indeed to be the Messiah but also the *Christos* (the anointed Son of God) and the *Kyrios* (Lord) who shared in the divine powers—"If you confess with your lips that Jesus is Lord and believe in your heart that God raised him from the dead, you will be saved" (Rom 10:9).

Gentile Christianity

The Hellenistic Jewish Christian movement brought Christianity into the larger Gentile world. The missionary center for Gentile Christianity was the city of Antioch in Syria where the community was established around 35 after the death of Stephen. Antioch of Syria (present-day Antakya in southeastern Turkey) had been incorporated into the Roman empire by Pompey in 64 B.C.E. as the capital of the province of Syria. This Asian outpost of Hellenistic civilization gained such prestige that it rivaled Alexandria and the other great cities in Europe and Africa.

> Now those who were scattered because of the persecution that arose over Stephen traveled as far as Phoenicia and Cyprus and Antioch, speaking the word to none except Jews. But there were some of them, men of Cyprus and Cyrene, who on coming to Antioch spoke to the Greeks also, preaching the Lord Jesus. And the hand of the Lord was with them, and a great number that believed turned to the Lord. News of this came to the ears of the church in Jerusalem, and they sent Barnabas to Antioch. When he came and saw the grace of God, he was glad; and he exhorted them all to remain faithful to the Lord with steadfast purpose; for he was a good man, full of the Holy Spirit and of faith. And a large company was added to the Lord. So Barnabas went to Tarsus to look for Saul; and when he had found him, he brought him to Antioch. For a whole year they met with the church, and taught a large company of people; and in Antioch the disciples were for the first time called Christians (Acts 11:19–26).

In proclaiming the Gospel among the Gentiles, Hellenistic Jewish-Christian missioners began using categories for interpreting Jesus and his message that would be comprehensible to an audience educated within Hellenistic culture. Christianity appealed to many of the Gentiles with its teaching on the resurrection of the body and the hope for the coming of a liberator. Jesus was presented as the divine Redeemer figure who descended to earth from a higher realm and then after accomplishing his mission ascended back to God. The followers of Jesus would in turn overcome death as Jesus did and come to share his glory. The eucharistic meal was understood as the principal means by which the believer became a sharer in the passage of Jesus from death to life.

I am the living bread which came down from heaven; if anyone
eats of this bread, he will live forever; and the bread which I shall
give for the life of the world is my flesh. . . . As the living Father
sent me, and I live because of the Father, so he who eats me will
live because of me (Jn 6:51, 57).

The Middle Period of First Century Christianity

Christianity, as it began to spread rapidly among the Gentiles, had
to face two major questions: first, the nature of its relationship to
Judaism, and, second, its relationship to the Roman empire. In establishing churches throughout the Gentile world, Paul was forced to
decide whether the converts to Christianity must first become Jews
and then follow the Jewish law after their baptism. The apostle to
the Gentiles decided that Gentile converts need not undergo adult
circumcision nor follow the prescriptions of Jewish dietary laws.
Paul's decision was confirmed by the apostles and elders of the Palestinian Jewish-Christian Church gathered at the Council of Jerusalem around 49. The fall of Jerusalem and the destruction of the
temple by the Roman army in 70 further separated Christianity
from Judaism. While maintaining continuity with its Jewish ori-

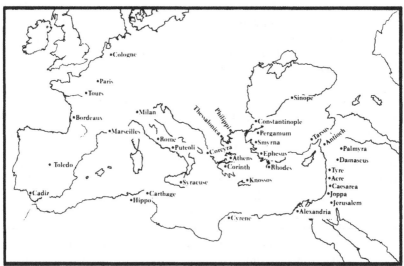

The Spread of Christianity

gins, Christianity would increasingly become a distinct religious movement with a profoundly Gentile identity.

The emperor Nero (54–68) blamed the Christians for the fire that devastated Rome in 64 and initiated a local and temporary persecution of the Christian community. Although Roman officials had previously tolerated Christianity as a sect within Judaism, they now came to see it as an independent religious movement which challenged many of the pagan values and beliefs of Greco-Roman culture.

The refusal of Christians to worship the genius of the emperor and the goddess Roma was viewed as a threat to the political stability of the empire. The strict ethical code of the Christian communities and their refusal to participate in the pagan aspects of civic life seemed to undermine the social unity that held the diverse peoples of the empire together. As alternative communities the Christians provoked the growing opposition of civic officials to their way of life which often resulted in periodic persecution on the local level.

During this phase of its development Christianity came to a deeper understanding of its identity and mission. A core of fixed beliefs began to take shape as the Christian movement assumed more distinctive characteristics.

Therefore remember that at one time you Gentiles in the flesh, called the uncircumcision by what is called the circumcision, which is made in the flesh by hands—remember that you were at that time separated from Christ, alienated from the commonwealth of Israel, and strangers to the covenants of promise, having no hope and without God in the world. But now in Christ Jesus you who once were far off have been brought near in the blood of Christ. For he is our peace, who has made us both one, and has broken down the dividing wall of hostility, by abolishing in his flesh the law of commandments and ordinances, that he might create in himself one new man in place of the two, so making peace, and might reconcile us both to God in one body through the cross, thereby bringing the hostility to an end. And he came and preached peace to you who were far off and peace to those who were near; for through him we both have access in one Spirit to the Father. So then you are no longer strangers and sojourners, but you are fellow citizens with the saints and members of the household of God, built upon the foundation of the apostles and prophets, Christ Jesus himself being the cornerstone, in whom the whole structure is joined together and grows into a holy temple in

the Lord; in whom you also are built into it for a dwelling place of
God in the Spirit (Eph 2:11–22).

Emergent Catholicism

By the last decade of the first century of the common era, Christianity was well on its way to becoming an institution with distinctive
religious literature, a specific set of credal beliefs and a community
with organized structures of ministry and leadership. Certain beliefs about the person of Jesus, his relationship to God and his mission formed the basis of unity among the various Christian communities. That unity flowed in a special way from the communal meal of
the Lord's Supper which the early Christians celebrated in their
house churches.

> The cup of blessing which we bless, is it not a participation in the
> blood of Christ? The bread which we break, is it not a participation
> in the body of Christ? Because there is one bread, we who are
> many are one body, for we all partake of the one bread (1 Cor
> 10:16–17).

Church order or structure developed around the person of the
bishop or elder who was seen as the leader of the Christian community. His special function was to preserve the true teaching handed
down from the apostles.

> This is why I left you in Crete, that you might amend what was
> defective, and appoint elders in every town as I directed. . . . For a
> bishop, as God's steward, must be blameless; he must not be arro-
> gant or quick-tempered or a drunkard or violent or greedy for
> gain. . . . He must hold firm to the sure word as taught, so that he
> may be able to give instruction in sound doctrine and also to con-
> fute those who contradict it (Tit 1:5–9).

During the last decades of the first century the early Christian
communities grew throughout Asia, across Asia Minor, in Greece
and in Italy. By 140 what had begun as a Jewish messianic movement in Palestine was now a distinctly Gentile Christian church
present in all parts of the Roman empire. Christianity was on the
threshold of its encounter with all aspects of Hellenistic culture and

the many political, social, and economic realities of the Roman world.

FOR FURTHER READING

Raymond E. Brown, *The Churches the Apostles Left Behind* (London: Geoffrey Chapman, 1984).

Richard J. Cassidy, *Jesus, Politics, and Society* (Maryknoll, N.Y.: Orbis Press, 1978).

Albert Nolan, *Jesus Before Christianity* (Maryknoll, N.Y.: Orbis Books, 1978). Nolan examines Jesus' options for a prophetic ministry and for the poor. He also situates Jesus and his mission both within the larger world of the Roman empire and the more immediate world of Palestinian Judaism. This approach influenced our presentation of the Jesus material.

Norman Perrin, *The New Testament: An Introduction* (New York: Harcourt Brace Jovanovich Inc., 1974). This is a good introduction and very readable. Perrin's description of the early phases of the development of the Christian Church helped shape our presentation.

9

Apostolic Fathers and the Apologists—Second Century Christianity

The Apostolic Fathers

The apostolic Fathers were early Christian writers who were either immediate disciples of the apostles or followers of those who had been immediate disciples of the apostles. Central to the role of the apostolic Fathers is their witness to the preaching of the apostles contained in the apostolic tradition. Clement of Rome's *Letter to the Corinthians,* the seven letters of Ignatius of Antioch and Polycarp's *Letter to the Philippians* are examples of this second level of Christian literature. Writing in *Koine* Greek, these authors imitated the literary style of the letters of Paul found in the New Testament.

Written out of pastoral concern for the handing on of the apostolic faith, these letters are theological witnesses to the life situation of various Christian communities in the early second century. For the apostolic Fathers, the norm of the Christian faith was the teaching of the apostles as formulated in the Gospels and now authentically taught by their legitimate successors—the bishops of the Church. These letters thus emphasized the significant role of the bishop in the community and the harmony that should exist between him and the other members of the Church. Ignatius of Antioch writes to the Christians at Tralles in Asia Minor:

Surely, when you submit to the bishop as representing Jesus Christ, it is clear to me that you are not living the life of men, but that of Jesus Christ, who died for us that through faith in his death you might escape dying.

It is needful, then—and such is your practice—that you do nothing without your bishop; but be subject also to the presbytery as representing the apostles of Jesus Christ, our hope, in whom we are expected to live forever.

Recognition is also given by the apostolic Fathers to the unique role or position of the Roman Church. Ignatius writes in his *Letter to the Romans:*

Ignatius, also called Theophorus, to the Church that has found mercy in the transcendent Majesty of the Most High Father and of Jesus Christ, his only Son; the Church by the will of him who willed all things that exist, beloved and illuminated through the faith and love of Jesus Christ our God; which also presides in the chief place of the Roman territory; a Church worthy of God, worthy of honor, worthy of felicitation, worthy of praise, worthy of success, worthy of sanctification, and presiding in love, maintaining the law of Christ, and bearer of the Father's name: her do I therefore salute in the name of Jesus Christ, the Son of the Father.

The apostolic Fathers see a close connection between true life in accord with the Gospel and orthodox teaching about the Eucharist as the center of Christian worship. Ignatius writes to the Church at Smyrna in Asia Minor around the year 110:

Observe those who hold erroneous opinions concerning the grace of Jesus Christ which has come to us, and see how they run counter to the mind of God! They concern themselves with neither works of charity, nor widows, nor orphans, nor the distressed, nor those in prison or out of it, nor the hungry or thirsty.

From Eucharist and prayer they hold aloof, because they do not confess that the Eucharist is the Flesh of our Savior Jesus Christ, which suffered for our sins, and which the Father in his lovingkindness raised from the dead. And so, those who question the gift of God perish in their contentiousness. It would be better for them to have love, so as to share in the resurrection.

To the Roman officials intent on preserving the civil order that was sustained by the public observance of pagan religion, Christianity posed a serious problem. By their refusal to participate in pagan worship and their choice of being an alternative community, Christians were seen as adherents of an illicit religion. As such they were guilty of a public crime and could be sentenced to death by Roman officials or could be the victims of mob violence. Christians were accused of being atheists because they did not worship the Roman gods, and their early morning or late evening celebration of the Eucharist in private houses led to the charges of immorality.

Those Christians who gave their lives by refusing to deny their Christian faith were called "martyrs" or "witnesses." The choice of death rather than any compromise in their loyalty to Christ as their Lord and to the Christian faith as their way of life made the martyr or witness a person of heroism and exemplary life. The account of the martyrdom of the apostolic Father Polycarp, around 155, testifies to the significance attached to martyrdom by second century Christians.

> But he alone is especially commemorated by everybody, and he is spoken of in every place, even by the heathen. For he proved himself not only a famous teacher, but also a notable martyr, whose martyrdom all desire to imitate, since it was on the model of the Gospel of Christ. Having overcome the unjust ruler by his endurance and thus having gained the crown of immortality, he rejoices with the Apostles and all the just saints and is glorifying God, the Father Almighty, and blessing our Lord Jesus Christ, the Savior of our souls and helmsman of our bodies, the Shepherd of the Catholic Church throughout the world.

The Apologists

While the writings of the apostolic Fathers were directed to edification and internal concerns of the Church, the next generation of second century Christian writers, the apologists, sought to defend Christianity through literary works directed to the broader Greco-Roman world. The apologists were defenders of Christianity who

98–117	117–130	138–161	
Persecutions under Trajan	Persecutions under Hadrian	Persecutions under Antoninus Pius	
c. 96	c. 125	c. 150	155
Clement of Rome	Gnosticism	Justin Martyr	Polycarp martyred

refuted the calumnies and vile rumors rampant among the pagan population.

One of the foremost of the apologists (the word comes from the Latin "apologia," meaning defense) was Justin Martyr. Born into a pagan family around 100, Justin became a Christian convert when he was an adult. Since he was a philosopher and a teacher by profession, he used these skills to defend the Christian faith against its critics. Fifty years later he wrote the following refutation of atheism and immorality in his *First Apology:*

> Thus are we even called atheists. We do proclaim ourselves atheists as regards those whom you call gods, but not with respect to the Most True God, who is alien to all evil and is the Father of justice, temperance, and the other virtues. We revere and worship Him and the Son who came forth from Him and taught us these things, and also the legion of good angels who attend Him and reflect His virtues, and the Prophetic Spirit, and we pay homage to them in reason and truth, and pass His doctrine on intact to everyone who wishes to learn it.

> We who once reveled in impurities now cling to purity; we who devoted ourselves to the arts of magic now consecrate ourselves to the good and unbegotten God; we who loved above all else the ways of acquiring riches and possessions now hand over to a community fund what we possess, and share it with every needy person; we who hated and killed one another and would not share our hearth with those of another tribe because of their (different) customs now, after the coming of Christ, live together with them, and pray for our enemies, and try to convince those who hate us unjustly, so that they who live according to the good commands of Christ may have a firm hope of receiving the same reward as ourselves from God who governs all.

Besides refuting the charges made against Christians and affirming the profoundly moral stance of believers, Justin also tried to help his pagan contemporaries understand the worship life of the Christian

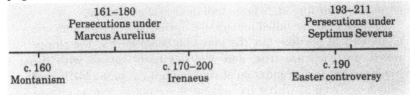

161–180		193–211
Persecutions under		Persecutions under
Marcus Aurelius		Septimus Severus

| c. 160 | c. 170–200 | c. 190 |
| Montanism | Irenaeus | Easter controversy |

communities. In his *First Apology* Justin offers the following description of the sacrament of baptism, which was the ritual whereby one
entered fully into the Christian community:

> Whoever is convinced and believes that what they are taught and
> told by us is the truth, and professes to be able to live accordingly,
> is instructed to pray and to beseech God in fasting for the remis-
> sion of their former sins, while we pray and fast with them. Then
> they are led by us to a place where there is water; and there they
> are reborn in the same kind of rebirth in which we ourselves were
> reborn: in the name of the God, the Lord and Father of all, and of
> our Savior, Jesus Christ, and of the Holy Spirit they receive the
> washing with water. For Christ said, "Unless you be reborn, you
> shall not enter the kingdom of heaven." . . . The reason for doing
> this, we have learned from the apostles.

Because the pagans had strange notions of what Christians did in
their celebration of the Eucharist, Justin presents the following account in his *First Apology:*

> And on the day which is called the Sun's Day there is an assembly of
> all who live in the towns or the country; and the memoirs of the
> apostles or the writings of the prophets are read, as much as time
> permits. When the reader has finished the president gives a dis-
> course, admonishing us and exhorting us to imitate these excellent
> examples. Then we all rise together and offer prayers: and, as I said
> above, on the conclusion of our prayer, bread is brought and wine
> and water; and the president similarly offers up prayers and thanks-
> givings to the best of his power, and the people assent with Amen.
>   Then follows the distribution of the Eucharistic gifts and the
> partaking of them by all; and they are sent to the absent by the
> hands of the deacons. The well-to-do who wish to give, give of their
> own free choice and each decides the amount of his contributions.
> The collection is deposited with the president, who gives aid to the
> orphans and widows and all who are in want through sickness or
> any other cause: he is also the protector of those in prison, of
> strangers from abroad, in fact, of all in need of assistance.
>   And this food is called among us "Eucharist," of which no one
> is allowed to partake but the one who believes that the things
> which we teach are true, and who has been washed with the
> washing that is for remission of sins and unto a second birth, and
> who is so living as Christ has enjoined. For not as common bread

and common drink do we receive these; but in like manner as Jesus Christ our Savior, having been made flesh by the word of God, had both flesh and blood for our salvation, so likewise have we been taught that the food which is blessed by the word of prayer transmitted from him, and by which our blood and flesh by assimilation are nourished, is the flesh and blood of that Jesus who was made flesh.

The writings of the apologists such as Justin Martyr helped the pagans of the Greco-Roman world to see Christianity as a desirable life-option that offered moral integrity, social concern and the support of the community bound by common bonds of faith, worship and structure.

Heresy and Controversy

Philosophical Heresy

As the Christian message moved into the Hellenistic world, it faced the challenge of Greek philosophy in general and of Gnosticism in particular. Gnosticism was a form of religious syncretism which utilized the language and imagery of Christianity to communicate its dualist understanding of reality. In Gnostic thought two co-equal principles guided human destiny, the principle of good associated with light and spiritual reality and the principle of evil associated with darkness and material reality. Human beings were a composite of the soul that was good and the body that was evil. The goal of life was to escape from the domination of the evil material body created by the gods of the Old Testament and return to the spiritual realm of light ruled by the unknown god of goodness.

The unknown god of goodness had sent Jesus the Savior into this evil world of matter with special knowledge or "gnosis" that would free his disciples from the power of matter and enable them finally to return to the realm of light. Because matter was evil Jesus only had the appearance of a human body and there would be no final resurrection of the body at the end of time as traditional Christian doctrine maintained.

Gnosticism as a sociological phenomenon was found in many areas or sectors of society. To some degree it represented a predilection for arcane or special knowledge which in turn conferred some kind of place or acceptance or power. One had identity by being part in some way of the divinity. In both Church and society Gnosticism appealed often to middle and lower class people who in fact would never make it to the upper echelons of society.

Since it made few moral demands on its adherents and had many apparent similarities to Christianity, Gnosticism in its many forms became a serious threat to orthodox or "right thinking" Christianity. A particularly dangerous form of the Gnostic heresy (wrong thinking) was the third century religious movement called Manichaeism. This dualist Christian heresy had its origins in the teachings of the Persian religious thinker Mani (216–276) and managed for a time even to ensnare an intellect as great as that of Augustine in the late fourth century.

Theological Heresy

Two kinds of theological heresy made their appearance in the second century. The first was Montanism, an extremist movement founded by a Christian leader in Asia Minor, Montanus, around 160. Opposed to what he considered to be the formalism and over-emphasis on the authority of the bishops of the Church, he maintained that he and his followers experienced the direct guidance of the Holy Spirit through visions and revelation. Montanism encouraged an ascetic or penitential life-style in anticipation of the imminent second coming of Christ and highlighted the prophetic dimension that had characterized an earlier phase of Christianity.

Montanism had a certain appeal to some Christians because of its emphasis on direct religious experience. It promoted that experience against a structured or institutional Christianity. Similarly it appealed to some people precisely because it saw the end of the world as near.

A second kind of theological heresy that concerned Christian leaders of the period was Monarchianism. This heresy emphasized monotheism or the oneness of God at the expense of the threeness of God as Father, Son and Holy Spirit, i.e., the Trinity. One of the principal advocates of Monarchianism was Sabellius (c. 195) who denied any real divinity or uniqueness to Christ by suggesting that Jesus was only one manifestation among the various forms assumed by the one God in the course of history. The appeal of Monarchianism rested on an innate fear of polytheism. Monarchianists solved the tension or mystery of the Godhead as understood by orthodoxy by ultimately denying the Trinity.

Jesus the Good Shepherd, from a mosaic in Ravenna, Italy.

Church Controversy

Certain controversies over questions of liturgical observance and
Church discipline also marked second century Christianity. The
chief issue of controversy was the correct date for celebrating Easter, the festival that commemorated the death and resurrection of
Jesus. The Christians of Asia Minor celebrated Easter on the fourteenth of Nisan (the first month in the Jewish calendar), the date
of the Jewish Passover. This was celebrated no matter what day of
the week it fell on. Western Christians in Europe always cele-

brated Easter on the Sunday following the fourteenth of Nisan. The debate became so heated that around 190 Bishop Victor of Rome was prepared to excommunicate the Christian communities of Asia Minor unless they adopted the Western pattern of celebrating Easter on Sunday. The moderating influence of Irenaeus, one of the great Church Fathers of the late second century, managed to bring a peaceful resolution to the situation by advocating that both customs be allowed to continue as valid differing traditions received from the apostles.

The point at issue, of course, in this controversy was that the Church in Rome received its tradition from the apostles Peter and Paul while the Church in Asia Minor received its tradition from the apostle John. The problem for many was that the great festival of the Christian community was celebrated on different days. Was agreement or a common celebration possible for all of the Christian community?

Irenaeus

Irenaeus of Lyons exemplifies the response of the Church to the heresies and controversies of the second century. In *Against Heresies* he teaches that true "gnosis" is to be found within the Church, where the bishops as successors of the apostles maintain the apostolic faith, and witness to the unity and love that are more important than prophecy.

> True knowledge is (that which consists in) the doctrine of the apostles, and the ancient constitution of the Church throughout all the world, and the distinctive manifestation of the body of Christ according to the successions of the bishops, by which they have handed down that Church which exists in every place and has come even unto us, being guarded and preserved, without any forging of Scriptures, by a very complete system of doctrine, and neither receiving addition nor (suffering) curtailment (in the truths which she believes); and (it consists in) reading (the word of God) without falsification, and a lawful and diligent exposition in harmony with the Scriptures, both without danger and without blasphemy; and (above all, it consists in) the pre-eminent gift of love, which is more precious than knowledge, more glorious than prophecy, and which excels all the other gifts (of God).

Historical Note

The early Church in a very real sense is the age of the "Fathers of the Church." This is a technical title for ecclesiastical writers of Christian antiquity. They are those writers of early Christianity who distinguished themselves for their orthodoxy of doctrine and holiness of life and have, therefore, been approved by the Chruch as special and significant witnesses to its faith. Broadly speaking there are three periods in the history of the Fathers of the Church. The first period extends roughly from 96 to 325 and saw the witness of the apostolic Fathers, the apologists and the first of the great thinkers or theologians of the Church. The apostolic Fathers included Clement of Rome, Polycarp and Ignatius of Antioch; among the apologists was Justin Martyr. The third century Fathers, such as Clement of Alexandria and Origen, presented the New Testament as a fulfillment of the Old Testament and often attempted in their writings to bridge the new revelation with Hellenistic philosophy.

The so-called "golden age" of the Fathers in the fourth and fifth centuries produced first-rate writers and thinkers. They inaugurated a period of creative Christian theology by attempting to penetrate and elaborate on the basic truths of Christianity. It was a period of Christian humanism which combined theological competence with secular learning and literary style. Such writers were Athanasius, Basil, Ambrose, Augustine of Hippo and Cyril of Alexandria.

The third or final period of the Fathers of the Church extends generally to the sixth or seventh century. While some notable writers stand out during this period in fact, the age of the Fathers was by then in decline. Perhaps one significant writer of the age was Isidore of Seville in Spain.

10

Expansion of the Church in the Mediterranean World— Third Century Christianity

The Christian Church emerged into the third century with a renewed sense of its mission to preach the Gospel in the world of Hellenistic culture and to act as a transforming influence within Greco-Roman society. Through its struggle with Gnosticism, as a philosophical heresy, and through facing its own internal theological controversies, the Church came to a clearer understanding of its own faith. At the end of the second century, that faith began to be expressed in creeds or official professions of beliefs promulgated by councils or used in the liturgy. These creeds reflected the apostolic teaching as that was presented in the writings that came to be the Christian Scriptures, the New Testament. The Church of the late second century began a process of establishing the New Testament canon or norm or official list, i.e., deciding which writings from the apostles' times were to be understood as definitive presentations of the Christian faith. The books of the New Testament were seen as the primary norm for the life of the Christian people.

As the formation of the creeds and the establishment of the canon of the New Testament provided a strong doctrinal or official basis for the Church of the third century, so the prominent role of the bishop as pastor and teacher in this period served as the focus of unity for the organizational aspects of the community. Thus the life of Christian communities of the third century was centered around their bishops, united by a common faith expressed in the creeds and motivated by the apostolic vision of Christian life found in the New Testament.

The developing doctrinal and organizational life of the Church expressed itself in art and architecture as well as in the formation of the canon and the creeds. From the earliest days of Christianity the faithful had worshiped in private homes. In the third century communities began to set aside houses specifically as places for common worship and charitable activity. These house churches did not differ in exterior appearance from the ordinary dwellings of a middle class Roman family. Rather it was the interior disposition of space and the wall paintings that gave the house church its specifically Christian character.

The remains of an early Christian house church built around 230

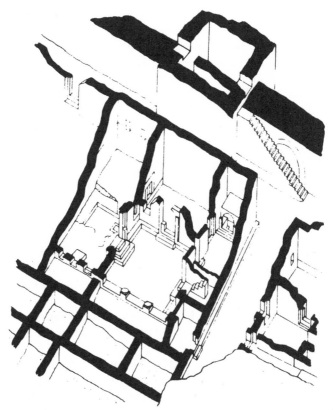

Cutaway drawing of a Christian meeting house in Dura-Europos around the year 230. The walls are painted with scenes of the Old and New Testaments. A step-in baptistry was located in the room at the upper right, beneath a canopy.

have been discovered at Dura-Europos, a town near the Euphrates River that was in the shifting border area between the Roman and Persian empires. The central court and dining room were used for the celebration of the Eucharist while an adjoining room at the northeast side of the house was transformed into a baptistry. Other rooms in the house were for the use of the bishop, the presbyters, the deacons and the deaconesses in their administrative, teaching and charitable activities. The pictorial decoration of the baptistry area shows scenes from the Old and New Testaments representing the salvation and new life that come from faith in Christ sealed by baptism.

Besides owning and decorating houses for worship, various communities in the third century also began to have distinctly Christian cemeteries. The most famous remains of these early Christian burial sites are the catacombs of Rome, subterrranean burial passages on the outskirts of the city. Here on wall niche tombs or in small chapels, the Christian artists of the third century painted scenes from the Old and New Testament and developed the system of symbols such as the anchor, the fish and the dove that have come to be an integral part of the artistic heritage of the Christian tradition. The patterns of growth and development in Rome, Alexandria and Carthage are indicative of the vitality that marked the alternative Christian communities of the third century.

The Church in Rome

From being a small Christian community composed of converted diaspora Jews in the first century, the Church of Rome had grown by the third century into a sizable community composed of Christians of diverse racial and linguistic backgrounds from all over the empire. Because many of these Christians were from the eastern half of the empire, Greek rather than Latin was the principal language of the Roman Church well into the third century.

The Christian community at Rome, however, not only had to face the problem of diverse ethnic membership but also the question of the very meaning of membership itself. Was the Church to be a community of perfectly formed saints as the Roman priest Hippolytus (170–236) believed or was it to be a school for training sinners in holiness as the bishops Zephyrinus (199–217) and Callistus (217–222) maintained? The answer, which was formative of the understanding of the Christian community as the Catholic or universal Church, was that the Christian community did indeed have saints among its members as the priest Hippolytus taught, but that it was also a place of universal hospitality and mercy where sinners, willing to undergo the process of conversion, were welcomed, as the Bishop of Rome, Callistus, maintained.

This Catholic or universal understanding of the Christian community as the home of both saints and sinners meant that the Church would continue to increase quantitatively while striving to deepen the faith commitment of its members qualitatively. At the time of Pope Cornelius (251–253) in the mid-third century the Roman Church had a very developed organizational structure that included, besides its bishop, forty-six priests, seven deacons, seven sub-deacons, and ninety-eight other minor officials. The community also supported over fifteen hundred widows and other persons in need.

Although the Christians of Rome experienced the full impact of the terrible persecution of the emperor Decius in the year 250, a strong community organization and their sense of universality enabled the Church to survive and emerge as an even stronger presence within the capital of the empire. The courage of the martyrs, the charitable activities of the community and the high moral standards joined with mercy, which marked the Church in Rome, had a profound effect upon the pagan population. The number of converts continued to grow and many thoughtful people began to think that any hope for the future would be found only in some reconciliation between Hellenistic culture and Christianity. The place where the fusion of Hellenistic culture and Christianity was first attempted was not, however, to be Rome, the political capital of the empire, but Alexandria, its greatest intellectual center.

The Church in Alexandria

The city of Alexandria in Egypt, founded in 332 B.C.E. by Alexander the Great, with its great library containing nearly a million volumes, was the intellectual capital of the Hellenistic world. The Greek population, the large Jewish population and the native Egyptian population had their own quarters in the same city, witnessing to the social complexity of this cosmopolitan center. The great first century Jewish thinker, Philo (20 B.C.E.–50 C.E.) had attempted in this complex environment to present Judaism in a Hellenistic form that would be acceptable to pagan intellectuals. Two Christian writers of the late second and early third centuries, Clement (150–215) and Origen (185–254), in a similar way sought to put Greek philosophy at the service of the Christian faith. They believed that philosophy could be the means whereby the Christian message could be introduced into the Hellenistic world. At the same time, the human wisdom which philosophy offered could provide an important contribution in trying to understand the mysteries of faith.

Third Century Fathers		
Rome	Alexandria	Carthage
Hippolytus (c. 170–236)	Clement (c. 150–215)	Tertullian (c. 160–225)
Minucius Felix (c. 175–230)	Origen (c. 185–254)	Cyprian (c. 200–258)

Clement of Alexandria

Born in Alexandria around 150, Clement, after his conversion to Christianity at an unknown date, traveled throughout the Mediterranean area seeking Christian wisdom. Returning to Alexandria at the beginning of the third century, he became a teacher within the Christian community. For Clement, Jesus Christ is the Word (Logos) who had come from the Father to teach us how to live so that we might share in his own eternal life, as shown in this passage from *Exhortation to the Greeks:*

Inasmuch as the Word was from the first, He was and is the divine source of all things; but inasmuch as He has now assumed the name Christ, consecrated of old, and worthy of power, he has been called by me the New Song. This Word, then, the Christ, the cause of both our being at first (for He was in God) and of our well-being, this very Word has now appeared as human. He alone being both, both one with God and one with us—the Author of all blessings to us; by whom we, being taught to live well, are sent on our way to life eternal. For, according to that inspired apostle of the Lord, "the grace of God which brings salvation has appeared to all, teaching us, that, denying ungodliness and worldly lusts, we should live soberly, righteously, and justly, in this present world; looking for the blessed hope, and appearing of the glory of the great God and our Savior Jesus Christ."

This is the New Song, the manifestation of the Word that was in the beginning, and before the beginning. The Savior, who existed before, has in recent days appeared. He, who is in Him that truly is, has appeared; for the Word, who "was with God," and by whom all things were created, has appeared. The Word, who in the beginning bestowed on us life as Creator when He formed us, taught us to live well when He appeared as our Teacher; that as God He might afterwards conduct us to the life which never ends.

In Clement's view we begin to share in eternal life through baptism, which is a rebirth and an illumination. The gift of God's grace in baptism initiates a process of dynamic growth in which the Christian is progressively identified with Christ, the giver of life and the teacher of integrity. He states in *The Instructor of Children:*

This is what happens with us, whose model the Lord made Himself. When we are baptized, we are enlightened; being enlightened, we become adopted sons and daughters, we are made perfect; and becoming perfect, we are made divine. "I have said," it is written, "you are gods and all of you the sons and daughters of the most High."

This ceremony is often called "free gift," "enlightenment," "perfection," and "cleansing," because through it we are completely purified of our sins; "free gift," because by it the punishments due to our sins are remitted; "enlightenment," since by it we behold the wonderful holy light of salvation, that is, it enables us to see God clearly; finally, we call it "perfection," as needing nothing further, for what more do we need who possess the knowledge of God?

Clement's doctrine of assimilation to Christ, the Word, has practical applications for daily life. Those who are advancing in their union with God through the study of Scripture should manifest in their conduct the Gospel values that have been the basis of their meditation. Clement emphasizes that Christians, as an alternative community within the war-oriented Roman empire, should be a people of peace and moderation. Every aspect of their behavior should witness their commitment to the Christian faith. Again, from *The Instructor of Children:*

We are educated not for war but for peace. In war, there is need for much equipment, just as self-indulgence craves an abundance. But peace and love, simple and plain blood sisters, do not need arms nor abundant supplies. Their nourishment is the Word, the Word whose leadership enlightens and educates, from whom we learn poverty and humility and all that goes with love of freedom and of mankind and of the good. In a word, through Him we become like God by a likeness of virtue. Labor, then, and do not grow weary; you will become what you dare not hope or cannot imagine.

Origen

The great Christian Scripture scholar, Origen, was born of Christian parents around 185. He functioned as a Christian teacher in the city of Alexandria until 232 when he went to Caesarea in Palestine where he also taught until his martyrdom in 254. Origen was a writer of great productivity who commented upon many books of the Bible and used Greek philosophy as a tool for deepening his understanding of Christianity. He believed that Christian intellectuals should continue the work of trying to understand the content of faith that was their heritage handed down from the apostles.

> Now it ought to be known that the holy apostles, in preaching the faith of Christ, delivered themselves with the utmost clearness on certain points which they believed to be necessary to every one, even to those who seemed somewhat dull in the investigation of divine knowledge; leaving, however, the grounds of their statements to be examined into by those who deserve the excellent gifts of the Spirit, and who, especially by means of the Holy Spirit Himself, should obtain the gift of language, of wisdom, and of knowledge: while on other subjects they merely stated the fact that things were so, keeping silence as to the manner or origin of their existence; clearly in order that the more zealous of their successors, who should be lovers of wisdom, might have a subject of exercise on which to display the fruit of their talents—those persons, I mean, who should prepare themselves to be fit and worthy receivers of wisdom. (*The Fundamental Doctrines*)

In his teaching Origen tried to present the Church's understanding that Jesus is both a man like us but also the Word of God. Although Jesus bore our sins on the cross and died in his humanity to save us, as God he was immortal and thus in the resurrection of

Jesus from the dead Christians have both forgiveness of their sins and the possibility of eternal life.

> Jesus, who died, is a man. Even in His own regard, He said: "But now you seek to kill me, a man who has spoken the truth." But while it is certainly a man who died, the Truth, Wisdom, Peace, and Justice, of whom it is written, "The Word was God," was not a man; and the God who is the Word, and the Truth, and Wisdom and Justice, is not dead. For the Image of the invisible God, the First-born of all creation is incapable of death.

> This man, the most pure of all living beings, bore our sins and weaknesses and died for the sake of the people; for neither did He know sin Himself,—but He was able to remove and to destroy and to blot out every sin of the whole world, all taken upon Himself, who did not sin—nor was deceit found in His mouth. (*Commentary on John*)

The Church in Carthage

The city of Carthage in North Africa was the center of Latin language and literature as Alexandria was the center of Greek language and literature. Carthage was a great maritime and commercial center whose proximity to Italy made it possible for the capital city of Rome to receive much of its grain from the fertile areas of North Africa. While Alexandrian Christian writers such as Clement and Origen sought an accommodation between Greek philosophy and the Christian Gospel, African Christians such as Tertullian (160–225) believed that philosophy and the Gospel were diametrically opposed. Tertullian writes:

> For philosophy is the material of the world's wisdom, the rash interpreter of the nature and the dispensation of God. Indeed heresies are themselves instigated by philosophy. . . . What indeed has Athens to do with Jerusalem? What has the Academy to do with the Church? What have heretics to do with Christians? Our instruction comes from the porch of Solomon, who had himself taught that the Lord should be sought in simplicity of heart. Away with all attempts to produce a Stoic, Platonic, and dialectic Christianity! We want no curious disputation after possessing Christ Jesus, no inquisition after receiving the Gospel! When we believe,

we desire no further belief. For this is our first article of faith, that there is nothing which we ought to believe besides. (*The Prescription of Heretics*)

Tertullian

Tertullian was born in Carthage of pagan parents and chose to make law his profession. After his conversion to Christianity as an adult, this brilliant controversialist and powerful writer gave the Latin West much of its theological outlook and vocabulary. Tertullian had an uncompromising attitude that saw Christianity as a struggle against the forces of untruth and moral evil. He advocated a militant Christianity that equally opposed heresy, Greek philosophy and pagan society. For Tertullian the martyr was the symbol of Christian life at its most heroic level, opposing all the values contrary to the Gospel.

> Crucify us—torture us—condemn us—destroy us! Your iniquity is the proof of our innocence. For this reason God permits us to suffer these things. In fact, by recently condemning a Christian maid to the panderer rather than to the panther (in the arena), you confessed that among us a stain on our virtue is considered worse than any punishment or any form of death. Yet, your tortures accomplish nothing, though each is more refined than the last; rather, they are an enticement to our religion. We become more numerous every time we are hewn down by you: the blood of Christians is seed. (*Apology*)

In the face of various Gnostic heresies, Tertullian saw the Church as the repository of revelation and the guardian of the apostolic faith that was now entrusted to the bishops as the authentic successors of the apostles.

> But if any heresies venture to plant themselves in the apostolic age, so that they may be thought to have been handed down by the apostles because they existed in their time, we can say: Let them exhibit the origins of their churches, let them unroll the list of their bishops, coming down from the beginning by succession in such a way that their first bishop had for his originator and predecessor one of the apostles or apostolic men; one, I mean, who continued with the apostles. For this is how the apostolic churches record their origins. The church of Smyrna, for exam-

ple, reports that Polycarp was placed there by John, the church of Rome that Clement was ordained by Peter. In just the same way the other churches produced men who were appointed to the office of bishop by the apostles and so transmitted the apostolic seed to them.

Let the heretics invent something, it will be useless to them. If their teaching is compared with the teaching of the apostles, the differences and contradictions between them will cry out that theirs is not the work of any apostle or apostolic man. (*The Prescription Against the Heretics*)

The ferocity of North African Christianity, personified in Tertullian, would soften its speech but not lessen its commitment to the Gospel in the more pastoral approach of the great mid-third century bishop of Carthage, Cyprian (200–258).

Cyprian

Cyprian was born of wealthy pagan parents in Carthage around the year 200. A gifted public speaker and civic official, he became a Christian at the age of forty-six. Two years later he was ordained to the priesthood and in 249, when he had been a Christian for only three years, he was chosen bishop of Carthage.

Both as leader of the Christian community and as a recent convert, Cyprian had a deep appreciation of the meaning of baptism and the commitment to holiness of life that it implied. In his *Commentary on the Lord's Prayer* he writes:

After this we say: "Hallowed be thy name," not because we wish for God that He be hallowed by our prayers, but because we seek from the Lord that His name be hallowed in us. Moreover, by whom is God hallowed who Himself hallows? But because He Himself said: "Be ye holy, for I am holy," we petition and ask for this, that we who have been sanctified in baptism may persevere in what we have begun. And for this daily do we pray. For we have need of daily sanctification.

We pray that this sanctification abide in us, and because our Lord and Judge warned the man who had been healed and quickened by Him to sin no more, lest something worse befall him, we make this petition with constant prayers, we ask this night and day that the sanctification and quickening which is assumed from the grace of God be preserved by His protection.

Because the early Christian communities took the baptismal commitment very seriously they believed that grave sins such as murder, adultery, and apostasy, i.e., the denial of the faith, could be forgiven only once by a long process of penance. Anyone guilty of serious sin had to confess the offense to the bishop and accept a penance that usually involved many years of prayer, fasting and almsgiving. When the years of penance were completed, the sinner then returned to the bishop, so that he or she could be absolved of the sin and readmitted to participation in the Eucharist.

When the emperor Decius in 250 ordered all the citizens of the empire under pain of death to offer public sacrifices to the pagan gods of Rome as a sign of civic loyalty, Christians faced a serious question of conscience. Many Christians committed apostasy either by actually offering the commanded sacrifice or by obtaining certificates which indicated that they had complied with the imperial order. In the rigorous atmosphere of North African Christianity, where martyrdom was the ideal, some Church leaders felt that apostates should not be admitted to penance but that they should be excommunicated or excluded from the Christian community for the rest of their lives. The demanding but also pastoral heart of Cyprian took a merciful approach to the apostates and offered them a second chance, as shown in his letter to Antonianus, a bishop in Numidia:

> But, if we find that no one ought to be prohibited from doing penance, to those entreating and imploring the mercy of the Lord, inasmuch as He is merciful and loving, peace can be given through His priests. The groans of those who mourn must be admitted and the fruit of repentance must not be denied to the sorrowful.

Cyprian himself died as a martyr in 258 when he was beheaded at the end of the great persecution of Valerian.

During the third century, the Church had grown numerically and had deepened its understanding of its own life and mission. The Church in Rome had developed a strong sense of catholicity or universality and recognized the importance of the unified organizational structure. In Alexandria the great thinkers Clement and Origen tried to reconcile the Christian message with the insights of Greek philosophy. At Carthage Tertullian and Cyprian maintained the truth of the Christian faith handed down from the apostles amidst all the challenges offered by heresy and pagan thought. But perhaps one of the greatest lessons learned by third century Christians was that the apostolic faith meant not only a commitment to martyrdom but also the capacity to show mercy when individuals failed. As Cyprian realized, and stated in that same *Letter to Antonianus*, the Church as an alternative community was a place of courage and hope because it was also a place of compassion and forgiveness.

> Do not think, dear Brother, henceforth that either the courage of the brethren is diminished or that martyrdoms fail because repentance has been mitigated for the lapsed and because hope of reconciliation has been offered to the penitents. The strength of the truly believing remains constant and integrity persists stable and strong among those who fear and love God with their whole heart. For a time of penance is allowed by us even to adulterers and peace is given to them. Yet virginity does not, on that account, fail in the Church, nor does the glorious design of continency languish through the sins of others. The Church flourishes, crowned with so many virgins, and chastity and modesty keep the tenor of their glory; nor is the vigor of continency destroyed because penance and pardon are mitigated for adulterers.

11

The Trinitarian Controversy—Fourth Century Christianity

Diocletian and Constantine

From the end of the persecution of Valerian in 260 until the reign of Diocletian (284–305), the Christian communities throughout the empire experienced growth, expansion and relative safety. Diocletian, however, was an autocratic ruler who felt that the vibrant Christian Church posed a political and social threat to the Roman empire at a time when it needed unity and cohesiveness. He decided to solve the Christian problem once and for all, a final solution, by unleashing an empire-wide persecution in which churches were destroyed, the Scriptures were burned and Christians were imprisoned and sentenced to death.

Although they suffered many martyrdoms and some defections, the Christian communities remained strong in their faith. The witness and organization of the Catholic Church prevailed, and the Diocletian persecution was unable to uproot the Christian faith from the empire. In fact Constantine (305–337), the successor of Diocletian, convinced that the future of the empire required a bold and new policy, decided to align himself with the Catholic Church. In 313 Constantine ended the state persecution of Christianity by the Rescript of Toleration. By granting the Church official toleration, Constantine started the process that would climax in Christianity becoming the official religion of the empire by the end of the fourth century.

Donatism

The persecution of Diocletian occasioned a prolonged schism or split
in the martyrdom-oriented Church of North Africa. Certain bishops
and priests had submitted to Diocletian's order, which required that
the books of Scripture be surrendered for burning to the public authorities. Donatus, a rigorist bishop in North Africa, subsequently
declared that bishops and priests who had succumbed to this imperial order were guilty of apostasy. Believing that the effect of the
sacraments depended upon the personal holiness and worthiness of
the minister, he maintained that bishops and priests guilty of serious sin such as apostasy could no longer validly administer the
sacraments.

Moving away from the policy of mercy and forgiveness adopted by
Cyprian, Donatus and his followers held out for an elitist under-
standing of the Church as a community of saints without serious sin.
Refusing any kind of compromise, the Donatists, the followers of
Donatus, broke off communion with the other Christian communi-
ties of the empire and set up their own church in opposition to the
Catholic Church in North Africa. This schismatic Donatist church in

The Birthplace of Donatism

North Africa posed a serious problem to the whole Christian community throughout the fourth century.

Augustine (354–430) was faced with the Donatist problem when he became bishop of the North African city of Hippo in 396. He devoted great energy and numerous writings to the Donatist schism, trying to convince these rigorist Christians to return to the Catholic Church. In his writings Augustine attempted to show the Donatists that the validity of the sacraments did not depend on the worthiness of the minister but rather upon Christ who freely granted his grace to Christians through the sacraments even when the minister was unworthy. But the greatest crisis faced by the Christian Church in the fourth century, as it became the official religion of the Roman empire, was not the Donatist schism but the Arian heresy.

Arius

The speculative, philosophical outlook developed by Clement and Origen at Alexandria in the third century led, in the fourth century, to a more systematic examination of one of the Church's central doctrines, its understanding of the nature of God. Christianity took its understanding of God primarily from the teaching of Jesus. In the Gospels, Jesus speaks of God as Father and of his relationship to God the Father as that of Son.

Similarly Jesus, especially in the Gospel of John, speaks of God dwelling in believers through and in the power of the Holy Spirit. The Father and the Son would send the Holy Spirit who would teach believers everything they needed to know for their life of faith and service.

> This much have I told you while I was still with you; the Paraclete, the Holy Spirit whom the Father will send in my name, will instruct you in everything, and remind you of all that I told you (Jn 14:25–26).

The Gospels speak of Christians as having a threefold relationship to God, Father, Son and Spirit. What does this relationship mean? Who is this Father–Son–Spirit God? Is the Christian God one or is the Christian God three? Can Judaic monotheism be preserved in the face of the Christian understanding of God as triune? Related to the question of the Trinity are two other issues: (1) Is Christ truly

God? (2) If Christ is not truly God, then how is the salvation of the human race accomplished?

The bishop of Alexandria in 318 A.D., Alexander, addressed the question of the Christian God in a sermon delivered to his clergy entitled, "The Great Mystery of the Trinity in Unity." The purpose of that sermon was to combat a unitarian understanding of the one God, while maintaining monotheism. A priest in the local church, Arius, vigorously attacked the bishop's theology because it did not seem to uphold sufficiently the distinctions within the Godhead. The stage was set for a great conflict that would spread beyond Alexandria and involve the whole Christian Church. Given the scriptural data, how was a Father–Son–Spirit God to be reconciled with the one God? Arius attempted to answer the question by offering an explanation that denied the true divinity of Christ. He proposed that when the person of Christ was spoken of as divine this meant that divinity was attributed to him simply as a way of describing his goodness. In fact, however, Christ, the Son, was a creature like us who was essentially different from the Father. Christ, the Son, was the greatest and the most perfect of all God's creatures, but he was not co-equal, co-eternal or of the same divine substance as the Father. Arius' teaching had popularity because it was simply an easier way to understand the mysterious reality of God. It preserved monotheism while asserting that Christ was indeed a great man.

Bishop Alexander condemned the teaching of Arius as heretical, and Arius fled to Asia Minor. This disunity on the theological level led to a broader crisis which threatened Constantine's vision of Christianity as an instrument for bringing unity to the empire. Chagrined to find disunity in the Church over the question of the nature of God, Constantine first tried to settle the dispute by letter. Finally the emperor summoned the bishops of the Church to an ecumenical council or worldwide meeting of bishops where they could work out a solution to the theological problem of the nature of God.

The Council of Nicaea

Roughly two hundred to three hundred bishops, mostly from the eastern half of the empire, gathered at the city of Nicaea in Asia Minor in 325. This first ecumenical or general council of the Church was dominated by the leadership of the emperor who was anxious for a speedy and definitive resolution of the issues raised by Arius.

Responding to the wishes of the emperor, the bishops formulated an official profession of faith called the Nicene Creed. In that creed the Church presented its understanding of the nature of God by declaring its belief in the divinity of Christ. Professing that Christ was "of one substance with the Father," the Council of Nicaea condemned as heretical the teaching of Arius which made the Son of God the greatest and highest of creatures but less than God.

Athanasius

The Catholic or orthodox position proclaimed at Nicaea was strongly defended by the successor of Bishop Alexander, Athanasius (295–373). Born of a wealthy Christian family and educated in the theological tradition of the Church of Alexandria, which employed philosophy to understand the mysteries of faith, Athanasius was a brilliant young man, thirty-three years of age, when he became bishop of Alexandria in 328. A dedicated supporter of the Council of Nicaea, which he had attended as a deacon in 325, Athanasius taught that Christ was of the same divine essence or substance as the Father although of distinct personality. If Christ were, in fact, less than the Father he could not have been the Savior of the human race. Christ, therefore, had existed from all eternity with the Father as co-equal, and consubstantial, that is, Christ was truly God. He writes in the *Discourses Against the Arians:*

> Whence the truth shows us that the Word is not of things originate, but rather Himself their Framer. For therefore did He assume the body originate and human, that having renewed it as its Framer, He might deify it in Himself, and thus might introduce us all into the kingdom of heaven after His likeness. For we would not have been deified if joined to a creature, or unless the Son were very God; nor would we have been brought into the Father's presence, unless He had been His natural and true Word who had put on the body. And as we had not been delivered from sin and the curse, unless it had been by nature human flesh, which the Word put on (for we should have had nothing common with what was

257–260 Persecutions under Valerian	303–313 Persecutions under Diocletian	305–337 Constantine
	c. 311 Beginning of Donatism	313 Christians win toleration

foreign), so also we would not have been deified, unless the Word who became flesh had been by nature from the Father and true and proper to Him. For therefore the union was of this kind, that He might unite what is human by nature to Him who is in the nature of the Godhead, and his salvation and deification might be sure.

The Arian Controversy: 325–337

With the condemnation of Arianism at the Council of Nicaea, most people, including Constantine, thought that the theological problem of the nature of God and the divinity of Christ was solved. Condemned by the council and exiled by the emperor, Arius himself became a forgotten man. In 330 Constantine symbolized his vision of the birth of a new unified Christian empire by moving his capital from the old Rome in Italy to the "New Rome," Constantinople at Byzantium on the Bosporus Sea between Europe and Asia.

The Arian movement, however, did not go away, since some Greek bishops such as Eusebius of Caesarea, who were supporters of Arius, were unsatisfied with the creed adopted at Nicaea. Eusebius indeed opposed the radical view of Arius that Christ was a creature and hence less than the Father. The bishop of Caesarea believed that Christ was eternally begotten of the Father and hence divine. But he opposed the view of the Council of Nicaea and the teaching of Athanasius that Christ was of the same essence or substance as the Father. To Eusebius that view destroyed the real difference between the Father and the Son as divine persons; he wanted to say that the Son was simply "like the Father" as God. Amid this new stage of the Arian controversy Constantine died (337) and was succeeded by his three sons.

The Arian Controversy: 337–361

Eventually Constantine's son Constantius became sole emperor. He supported what could be termed the "semi-Arian" position advocated by Eusebius of Caesarea. Athanasius, the great defender of Nicaea,

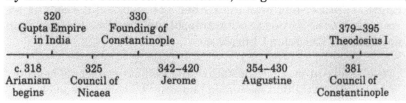

320 Gupta Empire in India	330 Founding of Constantinople			379–395 Theodosius I
c. 318 Arianism begins	325 Council of Nicaea	342–420 Jerome	354–430 Augustine	381 Council of Constantinople

believed that the semi-Arian position of Eusebius was merely a more sophisticated presentation of Arianism that ultimately rendered the divinity of Christ meaningless. In defense of the Catholic position, Athanasius appealed to the Bishop of Rome, Julius (337–352), for his assistance in opposing both the semi-Arians and the emperor Constantius who supported them. Arianism and the conflict engendered on the theological level now took on political overtones as a struggle between the emperor and the Bishop of Rome. Supported by the emperor, who was concerned for a unified Church in a unified empire, the brand of Arianism taught by Eusebius that the Son was simply "like the Father" continued to gain ground. The success of the semi-Arian position prompted the great biblical scholar, Jerome (342–420), to write: "The world groaned to find itself Arian."

The Arian Controversy: 361–381

From 350 onward a real effort was made to show intellectually that Athanasius' position that the Son is of the same identical essence as the Father was the only approach that did not destroy the orthodox faith as proclaimed at Nicaea. However, after 361 a new version of the problem emerged. The question now raised concerned the divinity of the Holy Spirit. Was the Holy Spirit divine? Was the Holy Spirit of the same substance as the Father or merely like the Father and the Son?

In 381 the Catholic emperor, Theodosius I (379–395), summoned the second ecumenical council which met in the capital city of Constantinople. The council reaffirmed the position taken at Nicaea that the Son is "begotten and not made" by the Father and hence that the Father and the Son are identical in essence. Thus the theological position of Eusebius of Caesarea and the like-minded theologians of the mid-fourth century was rejected as unorthodox or heretical. In addition the First Council of Constantinople affirmed that the Holy Spirit is truly God and of the same substance as the Father and the Son. To distinguish between the Son and the Holy Spirit, the Council described the Son as "begotten by the Father" and the Holy Spirit as "proceeding from the Father." The work of the council was embodied in the Nicene-Constantinopolitan Creed recited every Sunday in many Christian Churches.

We believe in one God, the Father, the Almighty, maker of heaven and earth, of all that is seen and unseen. We believe in one Lord,

Jesus Christ, the only Son of God, eternally begotten of the Father, God from God, Light from Light, true God from true God, begotten, not made, one in Being with the Father. Through him all things were made. For us men and for our salvation he came down from heaven: by the power of the Holy Spirit he was born of the Virgin Mary, and became man. For our sake he was crucified under Pontius Pilate; he suffered and died, and was buried. On the third day he rose again in fulfillment of the Scriptures; he ascended into heaven and is seated at the right hand of the Father. He will come again in glory to judge the living and the dead, and his kingdom will have no end. We believe in the Holy Spirit, the Lord, the giver of life, who proceeds from the Father and the Son. With the Father and the Son he is worshiped and glorified. He has spoken through the prophets. We believe in one holy catholic and apostolic Church. We acknowledge one baptism for the forgiveness of sins. We look for the resurrection of the dead, and the life of the world to come. Amen.

The ecumenical councils of Nicaea and Constantinople I offered definitive statements about the Christian understanding of the nature of God. Faith, which is a personal knowledge of God in Christ, had undergone serious theological reflection, and Greek philosophy had been employed in attempting to clarify the Church's understanding of the mystery of God. While the first two ecumenical councils had settled essential questions of the faith, the seeds of future disputes were also planted.

By the end of the fourth century, the Roman empire was nominally Christian, and the emperor was no longer the persecutor of an alternative community but the Christian leader of the kingdom of God on earth, as some described it. Since the emperor had convoked both councils to bring unity to the Church, the question of the role of the emperor deciding questions of doctrine and Church policy now came to the surface. Christianity faced a new and difficult problem: How was the Catholic Church to preserve the essential values of Christianity as it moved from being an alternative community in a pagan world to the status of the official religion of the Roman empire? That question seriously concerned many thoughtful Christians as the Church entered the fifth century.

12

Continuing Controversy and Church Structure—Fifth Century Christianity

At the beginning of the fifth century the Roman empire was nominally Christian. The transformation of Christianity from a persecuted alternative community at the end of the third century to the state religion of the empire at the end of the fourth century resulted in profound changes in the ways in which Christians lived and worshiped. Catholic Christianity within the Roman empire during the fifth century began to stabilize the worship patterns and the ministerial structures that would form the basis of its life for the next fifteen hundred years.

Church Buildings

The earliest Christian communities worshiped in private homes and later in community centers purchased by the Church. These "house churches" were ordinary buildings converted to a new use by the small urban communities of the Christian world.

Late in the third century and then with great rapidity after the Edict of Toleration in 313, the Church began to build large public assembly halls, called basilicas, for the use of the community. The basilica, which was the basic form of a Roman public building, was a large rectangular hall which terminated in a semi-circular extension, the apse, at the shorter end opposite the entrances. The hall itself, the nave, was divided into three aisles by two rows of columns. Arches supported the roof.

The apse of the basilica was reserved for the clergy, while the people or laity occupied the nave during services. The bishop, surrounded by his priests and deacons, presided at the first part of the Eucharist, the service of the word or scriptural readings, from his chair at the rear of the apse facing the congregation. For the second part of the Eucharist, the Lord's Supper itself, the bishop came forward to the altar, which served as the symbolic link between the clergy and the laity.

Besides the Eucharist the other great communal rite or sacrament of the Christian community was baptism as we know from Justin Martyr's account. During the fourth and fifth centuries the Church began to build baptistries adjoining the basilicas. Here, on the eve of Easter Sunday, new converts were initiated into the Christian faith by their baptism in the water-filled immersion pool at the center of the baptistry.

Sacraments and Worship

The two great sacraments of the early Church, baptism and Eucharist, were each celebrated in separate but adjoining buildings in the fifth century. Those who were doing public penance were restricted to the narthex or porch of the basilica until they had completed their

The Basilica

period of penance and were formerly readmitted to the Lord's Supper by the bishop on Holy Thursday, the Thursday before Easter Sunday. The other sacramental rites of the Church, ordination to the ministry, marriage and anointing of the sick, were also important aspects of the life of the members of the community.

Constantine had made Sunday, the day on which Christians celebrated the Eucharist together in memory of the Lord's resurrection, a public holiday. In the course of the fourth century, the Church began to develop a yearly cycle of feasts such as Easter, Pentecost and Christmas, which commemorated historical events in the life of Jesus and his earliest disciples. Those men and women who had died as martyrs, especially in the great persecutions of Decius and Diocletian, were honored each year on the anniversary day of their martyrdom by local Christian communities. The Sunday Eucharist, the memorial days of the martyrs and the daily morning and evening prayer services held in the great basilicas were at the heart of the worship life of fifth century Christians. But these services were not only important acts of worship for the Church; they were also the Christian replacement for the pagan worship once rendered to the Roman gods. By the fifth century all pagan worship had been forbidden since Christianity was now the official religion of the Roman empire.

The Clergy

By the beginning of the second century, the Christian community had a three-tiered structure of ministry: bishops, presbyters or priests and deacons. Each Christian community in any city of the empire was presided over by a bishop who was assisted by a college or group of presbyters and usually seven deacons, who cared for the economic and social service aspects of the Church's life. When Christianity became the established religion of the empire, the presbyters, who had been advisors and co-workers of the bishop, now became pastors of urban or rural churches called parishes. Each city had only one bishop, but by the fifth century there were many Christian communities or parishes in a city or an area. Each parish had a parish priest or pastor who was responsible to the local bishop. The parish priest took care of the spiritual needs of his people especially by celebrating the Eucharist, preaching, instructing converts and offering moral guidance. The many parishes over which the bishop presided came to be called a diocese, an administrative term borrowed from the Roman empire to indicate a specific geographic area.

Dioceses were further grouped into larger geographical units called provinces which were directed by metropolitans or bishops of major cities. By the middle of the fifth century, ecclesiastical provinces were placed under the supervision of one of the five most important bishops of the empire: the bishops of Rome, Alexandria, Antioch, Constantinople and Jerusalem. Among these five bishops, called patriarchs, one held a unique place and played a special role in the life of the Church: the Bishop of Rome.

The Bishop of Rome

Roman Catholic Christians trace their understanding of the unique role played in the Church by the Bishop of Rome to the New Testament. Especially do they look to Matthew 16:18:

> I for my part declare to you, you are "Rock," and on this rock I will build my Church and the jaws of death shall not prevail against it. I will entrust to you the keys of the kingdom of heaven. Whatever you declare bound on earth shall be bound in heaven; whatever you declare loosed on earth shall be loosed in heaven (Mt 16:18–19).

John 21:17, wherein Jesus commands Peter to feed his lambs and tend his sheep, is also considered an important scriptural passage for understanding the role of the Bishop of Rome.

The Catholic tradition understands, first of all, that Peter was called by Jesus to fulfill a unique function in the college of the apostles. Secondly, that unique role was not only a primacy of honor but also one of authority. Peter had a special function to play in the early Church, a function related to teaching and government.

Christ founded the Church to continue his mission of announcing, proclaiming and establishing the kingdom of God. Jesus provided a certain Church order or structure, at least in seminal form, in conferring on Peter a fullness of power. The powers or office conferred on Peter implicitly contained the provision for succession, i.e., to Peter's successors as Bishop of Rome.

Early Christian history attests to the general recognition of a primacy attached to the patriarchy of Rome. All other bishops as well as imperial authority saw Rome as a unique Church founded on the apostles Peter and Paul. Other patriarchal cities, Alexandria and Antioch, and later Constantinople and Jerusalem, looked to Rome as special. Most, however, saw Rome as enjoying only a primacy of honor—first among equals. This understanding later gave rise to division in the Church. Rome, however, viewed itself as unique in terms of both honor and jurisdiction. Early Christian literature, e.g., the Letter to the Corinthians by Clement of Rome (c. 100), expressed just such a view.

The role of the Bishop of Rome and his function in the Church gradually took on more and more significance. A theory of the papacy was first elaborated by the fifth century Pope, Leo the Great (440–461). Leo was one of the greatest administrators in the early Church and laid the foundation for an interpretation of the primacy of the Bishop of Rome. This interpretation lasted for the next sixteen centuries. Leo taught that the Bishop of the Roman Church had the right of primacy because as head of the Church, although unworthy personally, he was heir and successor to Peter. Peter enjoyed merit in recognizing the true reality of Christ, who, in turn, conferred the primacy upon him. While Peter's special unique merit could not be transmitted, his powers and office could. The powers given by Christ to Peter constituted, in fact, an office that was capable of being inherited. The Bishop of Rome, the Pope, in fact did not succeed a predecessor in the office but rather succeeded Peter in that office. So no tribunal or higher court could subject papal rulings to revision nor could there be an appeal to any higher court once the Pope had spoken.

The papacy in fact was seen as a monarchic institution, where the sum total of powers were in the hands of the Pope. Local bishops and other patriarchs did not participate in the papal plentitude of power. According to Leo the Bishop of Rome enjoyed supreme authority; the state exercised regal power but not supreme power. During the second half of the fifth century the imperial court at Constantinople made ever increasing claims. The court entered the area of faith and doctrine and began appointing bishops. Based on Leo's theory the papacy felt forced to challenge the government since it was the prerogative of the papacy, not the court, to address Christian life, doctrine and organization. For Pope Leo the emperor also held an office instituted by God, but as a Christian layman he belonged to the body of the faithful entrusted to Peter's successors.

The Christological Controversies

The fourth century Trinitarian controversy concerned the Christian understanding of the nature of God, that is, the relationship between the Father, the Son and the Holy Spirit. The theologians of the fifth century had to struggle with questions related to Christ. How was the Church to understand Christ's divinity, his oneness with the Father, as that related to his humanity, his oneness with us? Bishop Apollinarius of Laodicea, in Syria, was a friend and supporter of Athanasius, who strongly opposed the Arian position that lessened the divinity of Christ. In an attempt to avoid the undue separation of the human and divine in Christ he taught that Christ had a true body and soul but that the spirit in man was replaced in Christ by the Logos. The Logos, as the divine element, actively dominated the passive element, the body and soul, in the person of Christ. He stressed the divine in Christ that minimized his true humanity. In effect, Apollinarius denied the completeness of humanity in Christ. After 378 his teaching provoked a storm in the Christian community and his thought was condemned in 381 by the First Council of Constantinople.

Nestorius and Cyril of Alexandria

In April 428 the imperial court named Nestorius the new bishop of Constantinople. Previously, he had been a monk in Antioch and as such was strongly influenced by the theological school of that city. Nestorius believed in both a literal interpretation of Scripture and the validity of Aristotelian philosophy in helping to understand the faith. Nestorius, therefore, was at odds with the theological school of Alexandria and its bishop Cyril, a school which favored an allegorical interpretation of Scripture and the philosophy of Plato in interpreting the Christian faith. There was also political rivalry over questions of ecclesiastical jurisdiction between the patriarch of Constantinople and the patriarch of Alexandria.

Nestorius disliked the use of the word Theotokos, "God-bearer," as a name for Mary, and preferred to call her Christotokos, "Christbearer." This meant that Mary could not be called Mother of God, for she was only the Mother of the human side of Christ. Nestorius understood Christ to be a perfect man in whom human nature was somehow morally linked to the divine nature in a mechanical union rather than an organic union of natures. Because he maintained that Christ was a God-bearer rather than a God-man, he said that it was foolish to think of Christ when he was a baby two or three months old as God.

Nestorius' opponent in this controversy over the divine and human aspects of Christ was Cyril, bishop of Alexandria (412–444). In 428 Cyril attacked Nestorius' doctrine in a public letter and let it be known that Nestorius was threatening the integrity of the Christian faith by denying the true divinity of Christ.

In a second letter in 430 Cyril presented his own teaching that in Christ there was a difference between the divine nature and the human nature but they were both truly united in the one person of Christ. Thus one could truly say that God suffered and died on the cross, that a two month old infant was indeed God and that Mary could legitimately be called the Mother of God.

The Council of Ephesus

Finding that the emperor Theodosius II (408–450) was favorably disposed to Nestorius rather than himself, Cyril of Alexandria appealed to Rome and gained the support of Pope Celestine I (422–432). To settle the growing dispute the emperor agreed to call the third ecumenical council which met at Ephesus in Asia Minor in 431. At its outset the council had features of a tragic comedy. Bishop Cyril and his supporters arrived in Ephesus first during the middle of June and immediately excommunicated Nestorius and his followers. Four days later Nestorius' allies arrived and excommunicated Cyril and his associates; Nestorius chose not to come at all. Two weeks later at the beginning of July the legates of Pope Celestine arrived from Rome and allied themselves with Cyril. Since the two groups were now deadlocked, they appealed to the emperor Theodosius to help resolve the situation.

Supported by the emperor, the majority of the fathers of the council agreed that the teaching of the Catholic faith was that Christ was perfect God and perfect man by union of two natures in one person. The title of Mother of God was accorded to Mary since she was the mother of the one divine person existing in two natures. Although the council formally condemned Nestorius and his teachings, his followers continued their work in the eastern section of the Roman empire, carrying their version of the Gospel to Persia, India and even China.

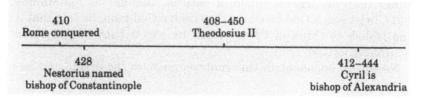

410
Rome conquered

408–450
Theodosius II

428
Nestorius named
bishop of Constantinople

412–444
Cyril is
bishop of Alexandria

The Aftermath of Ephesus

In reaction to the views of Nestorius, emphasis now began to be placed on the divinity of Christ to the detriment of his humanity. Eutyches, abbot of a monastery in Constantinople, in 448 insisted that after the incarnation the two natures of Christ, the divine and the human, were fused into one nature, the divine. The teaching of Eutyches ended the period of truce that had been established after the Council of Ephesus between the party of Alexandria led by Bishop Cyril and the party of Antioch led by Bishop John.

Once more the emperor Theodosius called a general council to meet at Ephesus in 449. Pope Leo the Great (440–461) sent delegates to represent him at the council. They carried a doctrinal statement called the "Tome" which insisted on the abiding character of the two natures in Christ as God and man without any fusion after the incarnation.

The supporters of Eutyches, who came to be known as monophysites or proponents of a single divine nature in Christ, took over the council and condemned those who taught that there were two natures in Christ as Pope Leo's Tome maintained. Because of its violence and heterodox teaching, this gathering is not considered a true ecumenical council but came to be know rather as "The Robber Synod of Ephesus."

The Council of Chalcedon

In July 450 the emperor Theodosius II fell from his horse and died. He was succeeded by his sister, Pulcheria, who took control of the empire and married a general, Marcian (450–457). The imperial couple summoned a new general council, the fourth, to meet at Chalcedon outside Constantinople in 451. The council taught that in accord with Scripture Jesus Christ was truly God and truly man, possessing two natures, human and divine, which were joined without confusion by the incarnation.

Many Eastern Christians refused to accept the decision of the Council of Chalcedon and separated themselves from the Church of

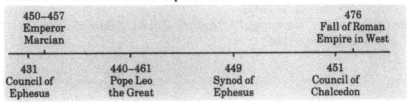

450–457 Emperor Marcian			476 Fall of Roman Empire in West
431 Council of Ephesus	440–461 Pope Leo the Great	449 Synod of Ephesus	451 Council of Chalcedon

the Empire. Monophysite Christians dominated the Coptic Church in Egypt, the Abyssinian Church in Ethiopia, the Jacobite Church in Syria and the National Church in Armenia.

At Chalcedon the assembled fathers acknowledged the orthodox character of Leo's Tome and even declared that "Peter had spoken through Leo." The teaching of Pope Leo was evident in the definition of faith offered to the Christian world by the council:

> Wherefore, following the holy fathers, we all with one voice confess our Lord Jesus Christ one and the same Son, the same perfect in Godhead, the same perfect in manhood, truly God and truly man, the same consisting of a reasonable soul and a body, of one substance with the Father as touching the Godhead, the same of one substance with us as touching the manhood, like us in all things apart from sin; begotten of the Father before the ages as touching the Godhead, the same in the last days, for us and our salvation, born from the Virgin Mary, the Theotokos, as touching the manhood, one and the same Christ, Son, Lord, Only-begotten, to be acknowledged in two natures, without confusion, without change, without division, without separation; the distinction of natures being in no way abolished because of the union, but rather the characteristic property of each nature being preserved, and concurring into one Person and one subsistence, not as if Christ were parted or divided into two persons, but one and the same Son and only-begotten God, Word, Lord, Jesus Christ; even as the Prophets from the beginning spoke concerning him, and our Lord Jesus Christ instructed us, and the creed of the fathers was handed down to us.

FOR FURTHER READING

Henry Chadwick, *The Early Church* (New York: Penguin Books, 1967).

W. H. C. Frend, *Saints and Sinners in the Early Church* (Wilmington, Delaware: Michael Glazier, 1985).

Fabrizio Mancinelli, *Catacombs and Basilicas: The Early Christians in Rome* (Firenze: Scala, 1981).

Boniface Ramsey, *Beginning To Read the Fathers* (Mahwah, New Jersey: Paulist Press, 1985).

13

Augustine of Hippo

The Life of Augustine

The life of Augustine coincides with the end of the classical era and the beginning of the Middle Ages. He was a man who looked back to the past as well as one who predicted the future, and his life would become a paradigm for subsequent Christian understanding of the individual's journey to salvation. As one of the greatest thinkers and saints of all times, he spent his life trying to answer the basic questions of human existence. How does one find true happiness? How is one saved? What is the role of others in our finding happiness and salvation?

Augustine's life manifests the exterior geographical journey of one who was trying to find the right place to establish a home and engage in a profession. It also reflects the interior spiritual journey of one who was looking for some meaning to his life and for peace of heart. Born in Tagaste, North Africa, in the year 354, Augustine received an excellent classical education in the city of Carthage. Upon completion of his formal studies, he left Carthage and became a teacher first at Rome and later at Milan in northern Italy. Augustine's early life was marked by the freewheeling life-style that characterized the student community in Carthage. For many years he lived with a woman whom he never married and by whom he had a son, Adeodatus, a name meaning "a gift from God." Augustine's mother Monica finally succeeded in breaking up the relationship but only at a much later date.

In his student days he was also concerned about the question of meaning in his life. The North African Christianity practiced by his mother had no appeal for him, since it struck him as simplistic and unsophisticated. The dualist vision of reality offered by the Manichaean religion seemed to offer an initially satisfying response to

Augustine's quest, and for nearly ten years he was an adherent of this sect.

As the residence of the Western Roman emperor, Milan was an important cultural and intellectual center during this time. Ambrose, the bishop of Milan, became a significant person in Augustine's development by introducing him to the philosophy of the neo-Platonists. This important philosophical system, developed by Plotinus in the previous century, emphasized the unity of God and the search for the true, the good and the beautiful as the basis for human existence. Augustine was immediately drawn to this view of reality because it was far more satisfying intellectually and personally than the dualism of Manichaeism. Ambrose also introduced Augustine to a more satisfying method of interpreting Scripture. The new intellectual environment provided by Ambrose paved the way for Augustine to open his heart to the grace of God and to make the necessary moral decisions required for his conversion to Catholic Christianity. Augustine and his son Adeodatus were baptized by Ambrose during the Easter vigil in 387.

Fired with zeal to devote the rest of his life to study and contemplation, Augustine returned to North Africa and established a small monastery there. His goal was to spend his time searching for a deeper understanding of the Christian faith through prayer, work and community life. Such, however, was not to be the case. The genius of Augustine and his commitment to Catholic Christianity led to his ordination to the priesthood in 391 and his election to the episcopacy as bishop of Hippo in 396.

Bishop Augustine was a true pastor and theologian who was concerned for the salvation of his flock and for proclaiming the Gospel. In his work of handing on the apostolic faith to his people and attempting to explain the meaning of the Gospel, Augustine made a significant contribution to the developing theology of the Latin-speaking West. In responding to the many theological questions and socio-political issues facing the Church, he composed a vast body of literature, over twelve hundred works, covering a great variety of topics. Because his work was often done in the heat of debate with his opponents, Augustine's writings are sometimes difficult to follow

354	387	396	397–401
Augustine born	Baptized by Ambrose	Made bishop of Hippo	*Confessions* written

as he moves first in one direction and then in another. In the midst of controversy an author often overstates his case and emphasizes certain factors that would be more carefully balanced in a less intense situation. To understand Augustine, then, one must try to understand the setting of the world in which he tried to be a faithful pastor, preserving his flock in the truth of the Catholic faith.

The World of Augustine

The social setting or horizon for Augustine's ministry and writing was the crumbling Roman empire of the early decades of the fifth century. The fall of the city of Rome to invading Germanic tribes in 410 became the symbol of the end of the classical age both to the Christian majority and to the pagan minority that remained in the empire. The idea of eternal and invincible Rome, which had given meaning and purpose to the lives of the citizens of the empire for hundreds of years, was now shattered. Because many Christian writers had interpreted the conversion of the empire as the beginning of God's kingdom on earth, the fall of the city of Rome was especially devastating and difficult to understand. In his classic work, *The City of God,* Augustine tried to address this problem by placing it in the broader context of God's overall plan of salvation.

Another set of issues faced by Augustine related to philosophical and theological questions concerning the doctrine and life of the Church itself. In his preaching and teaching, the bishop of Hippo addressed four major movements which threatened the integrity of the apostolic faith. First, he struggled with the Donatists who maintained that the validity of the sacraments depended upon the personal holiness of the minister. Augustine rejected this elitist view of the Church and the sacraments by maintaining that Christ was the primary minister of the sacraments who assured their validity as instruments of God's grace.

Second, Augustine wrote against the views of the Manichaean dualists which he had held himself as a young man. Opposing the Manichaean depreciation of matter in general and the human body in par-

	410 Rome conquered	418 Goths rule France	
c. 399 Battles Manicheans	411 Debate with Donatists	413–427 *City of God* written	430 Augustine dies

ticular as a creation of the evil principle, Augustine taught the unity of creation and its goodness flowing from the love of God the Creator.

Third, Augustine battled the British monk Pelagius who believed that a person could obtain salvation through good works alone without needing God's grace. From his own experience of the absolutely essential character of God's grace in the process of overcoming sin, Augustine declared that God's grace was necessary at every moment in human life because no one could achieve salvation by one's own efforts alone.

Finally at the end of his life, the bishop of Hippo had to answer those who promoted a moderate version of Pelagius' doctrine known as semi-Pelagianism. Against these well-meaning individuals who misunderstood the role of human cooperation in the process of personal salvation, Augustine taught that even the initial desire to change one's life or to accept the Christian faith was the work of God's transforming power of love or grace.

The fall of the city of Rome and the four theological debates which we touched on formed the social and religious background for Augustine's preaching, teaching and writing. His extensive body of writings constituted the core of Latin-speaking Christian theology in the West for the next thousand years. Augustine's world-view offered an understanding of human life which was to dominate Christian thinking. His presentation of Christian life would be the frame of reference within which people understood themselves and the world around them throughout the Middle Ages.

The Theology of Augustine

Augustine's theology might seem somewhat pessimistic today, but it must be remembered that it was highly influenced by his own struggle against sin in his personal life and his experience of the absolute gratuity of God's grace in his conversion. For the bishop of Hippo men and women are born into a condition of radical alienation from God, called original sin, which powerfully influences, if not determines, the course of their lives. Salvation is possible only by the healing power of God's grace which re-creates the person and makes good works part of the redeemed individual's life. Augustine's anthropology emphasizes the depravity from birth and the inclination to selfishness and sin of the human person on the one hand while indicating the desire of God to cure and restore the human race through the redemptive work of Christ on the other. How does one achieve salvation? How does the human community arrive at the proper destiny of its journey? Augustine answers in his *Confessions*, Book X, that the spiritual sickness of both the individual and the community requires the healing power of God's grace to reach the goal of the human journey—eternal salvation.

> Do you, my inmost physician, make clear to me with what profit I do these things. For when they are read and heard, these confessions of my past sins—which "you have forgiven and covered over," so that you may make me blessed in you, changing my soul by faith and your sacrament—stir up the heart. Then it will not sleep in despair and say, "I cannot," but it will awaken in love of your mercy and in your sweet grace. Through this grace whosoever is weak is strong, when by its means he comes to know his own weakness.

Augustine sees the fact and power of sin operative in the immoral conduct and the human structures of the society in which he lives. Men and women who refuse to live by the healing power of grace and choose rather to form a community characterized by egoism and exploitation constitute "the City of Man." Those healed by grace who seek to build a new society based on the love and forgiveness proclaimed in the Gospel form "the City of God." In his great work *The City of God* Augustine taught that the city of Rome fell because it was not truly living the values of the Gospel and thus was in reality "the City of Man." Although the perfect "City of God" can be realized only in the final happiness and eternal salvation of heaven, by participating in the sacraments and the Church's concern for others, men and women while on earth can already share partially in the community of grace that is "the City of God." Augustine allegorized on the parable of the good Samaritan. Men and women because of original sin were the wounded victim by the side of the road. The good Samaritan was Christ, who rescued and healed the wounds of humanity. He did that by applying the medicine of the sacraments and bringing the wounded person to the inn of the Church.

Because Augustine's theology was heavily influenced by neo-Platonic thought, he was somewhat pessimistic about the human situation in time and in the material world. Since the ideal world of the "City of God" was achieved in its perfection only in heaven, life in this world was filled with trials, temptations and the constant experience of imperfection. The good which men and women know in this life is only a pale reflection of the goodness and joy of heaven, our true home.

It is difficult to overstate the enormous influence that Augustine has had upon the development of Western civilization. His world view would provide the context for understanding personal and communal Christian destiny for the next thousand years. Only in the thirteenth century would Augustine's neo-Platonic understanding of Christianity yield somewhat to the Aristotelian understanding of Christian life proposed by Thomas Aquinas. Because he was a pastor as well as a theologian, his influence has been felt by both ordinary Christians and Church leaders even to the present day. As he lay dying in the year 430, Augustine's city of Hippo was under siege by one of the fiercest of the Germanic tribes, the Vandals. The voice of Augustine, the great Father of the early Church and the forerunner of the Middle Ages, who sought to protect and defend, to lead and to teach, to comfort and to strengthen his family, the Church, reaches to all times and places, as we again see in Book X of his *Confessions:*

> Too late have I loved you, O Beauty so ancient and so new, too late have I loved you! Behold, you were within me while I was outside: it was there that I sought you, and, a deformed creature, rushed headlong upon these things of beauty which you have made. You were with me, but I was not with you. They kept me far from you, those things which, if they were not in you, would not exist at all. You have called to me, and have cried out, and have shattered my deafness. You have blazed forth with light, and have shone upon me, and you have put my blindness to flight! You have sent forth fragrance, and I have drawn in my breath, and I pant after you. I have tasted you, and I hunger and thirst after you. You have touched me, and I have burned for your peace.

14

The Rise of Monasticism

The word "monk" comes from the Greek word "monos" meaning "alone" or "solitary." Christian usage of the word "monk" derives from the fourth century. At first it meant principally a hermit; later it was applied to anyone who "left the world to follow Christ." At a later date the word covered all religious, men and women, as a distinctive group within the Christian community, as well as different forms of religious life such as the friars.

Antony and Pachomius

The monastic movement began in the Egyptian desert in the last decades of the third century. Antony (251–356), a young Egyptian Christian, experienced a call from God to sell all that he possessed and to use the proceeds for the poor. He then withdrew into the Sahara Desert where he lived alone engaging in prayer and manual labor. After long years of solitary existence, Antony found himself surrounded by a number of disciples. They had heard of his fame as a holy man and wished either to imitate his life-style or to obtain his advice about their lives. Antony thus became the model both for hermits and for those who wished to live a more communitarian form of monasticism.

At a point in time contemporary with the early hermit days of Antony, the emperor Diocletian (284–305) demanded that Christians renounce their faith as a sign of loyalty to the Roman empire. Many Christians refused and were martyred in the great persecution of 303–312, choosing to give up their lives rather than renounce their baptismal commitment to Christ.

When Constantine ended this persecution by the Edict of Toleration in 313, he began the process of making Christianity the state religion. Many Christians objected to the blending of Church and state, believing that the Church should not be identified with the current culture but should be an alternative community critical of the status quo. Individuals who opposed this blending of the secular and the sacred saw Antony's withdrawal into the desert as a pattern of life that would continue to allow Christianity to be an alternative form of community. Christians who chose this life option, the monks, became a cultural counter-sign protesting the identification of the Church with the Roman empire.

Besides setting limits on the blending of the sacred and the secular, the monks also sought to witness to the absolute demands of the Gospel and the kingdom of God. The monks reminded the Church that loyalty to Christ and to the standards of Christian conduct, embodied in the Gospel, had to be the most important priority in the life of every believer. In an age when Christians were no longer asked to shed their blood as martyrs in loyalty to the ideals of the Gospel, the monks became bloodless martyrs who proved their loyalty to Christ by a counter-cultural style of Gospel living.

The men and women who embraced the monastic life-style were not usually priests but lay people who were motivated by a radical concern for their own salvation. Because they longed for integrity and authenticity, they left the world in search of something that would fulfill them and complete them as persons. They believed that Christ and a life led in strict conformity to the ideals of the Gospel were the only realities that could bring true happiness. Monks, therefore, were concerned with personal perfection—"If you would be perfect, go sell what you have and give to the poor, and you will have treasure in heaven; and come, follow me" (Mt 19:21).

Monks left the world to live in solitary places, e.g., the desert or the isolated areas of a region. Since the things of the world were seen as distractions to their single-minded quest for God, they hoped to meet God in solitude. There, monks lived a very simple life of prayer, penance and work. Penitential practices or asceticism such as fasting or long hours of prayer were means whereby the monk gained self-control and subdued the passions. By dying to the old self marked by sin and selfishness, the men and women of the desert hoped to be reborn in Christ as new persons already sharing in the peace of heaven while here on earth.

Pachomius, a contemporary of Antony, began his monastic career as a hermit. However, he had great organizational skills and put them to good use in creating a new form or style of monasticism—life together in an organized community. Recruits came by the hundreds from all over the eastern half of the empire to the monastery

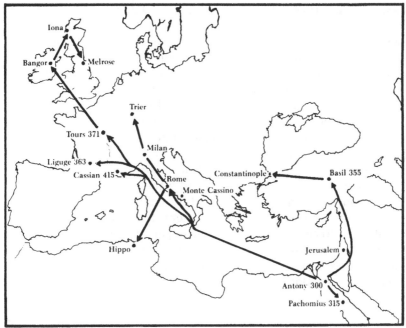

The Spread of Monasticism

which he established on the banks of the Nile. Pachomius developed a rudimentary rule which called for a communal sharing of goods, celibacy and obedience to the superior of the monastery. Abandoning his personal preferences in the spiritual life, the monk was expected to conform to a communal pattern of life that included public prayer and manual labor.

Over the years Pachomius' monastery grew into a small town where several thousand monks resided. Divided into small groups or communities according to their skills, e.g., farmers and bakers, they worked together for the essential needs of the whole community. This new form of monastic life was to serve as the primary pattern that would be developed and perfected by subsequent leaders of the movement.

Basil the Great

Basil the Great (330–379) founded a monastery in Asia Minor that embraced the essential features of Pachomian monasticism such as common life, liturgical prayer and manual labor. However, Basil's monastery also engaged in a ministry of social service. The monks took care of the sick and orphans and offered help to the poor and workshops to the unemployed. Basil's rule placed less emphasis on great feats of penance and stressed works of charity instead. Because of his profound influence on the development of monasticism within the Byzantine empire and later in Russia, he is known as the "Father of Eastern Monasticism."

In Egypt, Syria, Palestine and Asia Minor the essentials of monastic life, as well as numerous variations, were developed over a period of roughly one hundred years. A developed liturgical life, a theory of monastic community government and a theological understanding of the elements of monasticism itself were all the results of the first century of this new Christian movement. In the centuries that followed monasteries came to play an important role in the broader society of the Christian empire because of their size, their centers of learning, their involvement in social welfare and their successful economic institutions.

Evagrius and Cassian

One of the most influential writers and theologians of the early Christian monastic experience was Evagrius Ponticus (346–399). Deeply influenced by neo-Platonism and by Origen, this brilliant intellectual sought to understand the spiritual life in an ordered and systematic way. He tried to relate certain sins or evil tendencies to various aspects of the human personality and spoke of the eight basic sins (the ancestors of the medieval notion of seven capital sins): gluttony, luxury, love of money, despair, anger, pride, vainglory and distaste for spiritual things. Evagrius saw prayer in its highest form as a wordless mental act, without any image of God supplied by the imagination.

Another outstanding writer of the monastic movement was John Cassian (360–435), a monk trained in Palestine and Egypt. In 415 he organized a monastery for men and a convent for women near Marseilles, France. In his book *The Institutes* he carefully described

313		385
Edict of Toleration		Buddhism in China

251–356	330–379	360–435
Antony	Basil the Great	Cassian

the order or life-style that should characterize a religious community. In another book, *The Conferences,* he related his discussions with famous monks of the East in an attempt to articulate the inner journey of the spiritual life more clearly. The exterior and interior systematization of the monastic life established by Cassian was very significant for Western monasticism in general and for Celtic or Irish monasticism in particular.

Celtic Monasticism

Monasticism seems to have begun among the Celts in Ireland in the late fifth or early sixth century, although very little is known of its early history. Legend attributes Celtic monasticism to the influence of Patrick even though there is no certainty that he ever founded a monastery or was himself a monk. Celtic monasticism was characterized by a rigorous asceticism as well as by a love for scholarship. Fifth century Ireland was a tribal society without large cities. Monasteries exercised a great influence on the life of both Church and society. Irish monks often practiced penance or asceticism by voluntarily going into exile, leaving their homeland to wander in far places preaching the Gospel of Christ.

Patrick (c. 389–461) was probably born in Roman Britain. The details of his life are sketchy. At the age of sixteen Patrick was seized by raiders and sold as a slave in Ireland. After six years he escaped and eventually reached home. During his captivity he had deepened his religious and spiritual life and became convinced that he was called to return to convert Ireland to the true faith. He returned in 432 as bishop and spent the next thirty years of his life preaching and ministering to the Irish people. He influenced a number of important chieftains and through them was instrumental in converting the Irish people. Patrick encouraged scholarship and learning as well as the penitential life. He communicated the priority and importance of going on mission to spread the faith. Celtic monks during the so-called dark ages of Europe were found in many places on the European continent, preserving scholarship and establishing monasteries.

410 Visigoths sack Rome	481, Clovis King of Franks		
389–461 Patrick	480–547 Benedict	525 Monte Cassino	817 Rule of Benedict

Benedict

By the fifth century the number of hermits and monks was increasing rapidly all over the Western Roman empire. Many monasteries, however, were totally independent of each other and often lacked a permanent spiritual leader or stable monastic rule to guide their daily lives. An Italian monk, Benedict of Nursia (480–547), composed a rule—the Rule of St. Benedict—which was eventually to become the normative rule for the Western monastic movement. Although he himself never founded a religious order in the strict sense of the word, he is considered the patriarch of Western monasticism and the founder of the Benedictine family of religious men and women.

Benedict, whose holiness was manifest in his practical and humane vision of monastic life, composed a rule that emphasized charity and simplicity. The Rule of St. Benedict understands the monastic community as a family in which individual brothers or sisters

Benedict *(after a fresco at Monte Cassino)*

have dedicated themselves to renewal and rebirth in Christ. Living together in community under the authority of a religious superior, an abbot for men, an abbess for women, monks and nuns promised obedience to the lawfully chosen leader who ruled for life. In surrendering their free choice by obedience to the common good, Benedictine men and women sought to serve the entire monastic family as it journeyed collectively to God. The monastic schedule of prayer and work, "ora et labora," sought to unite men and women with God through the routine and ordinary tasks of daily life.

Under Charlemagne's son, Lewis the Pious (778–840), Benedict's rule became normative for all the monasteries of Western Europe in 817. The monastic movement launched by Benedict at Monte Cassino in Italy around the year 525 became one of the most significant factors in the development of Western civilization in the Middle Ages.

The Church always experiences tension between its call to live the ideals of the Gospel and the reality of life in a sinful and broken world. Throughout its history the Church has always measured itself against the Gospel standards described in the New Testament. At the same time, especially after the conversion of Constantine to Christianity, the Church developed institutions and bureaucracies necessary to survive and continue in any civilization. Monasticism has served as a constant challenge to the status quo of the post-Constantinian Church by offering the critique of a pattern of life that was radically committed to witnessing the Gospel. Monks and nuns have ever been intent on leaving the world to surrender totally to the demands of the Gospel and the proclamation of the kingdom of God.

Initially monasteries offered an alternative life-style to numerous men and women who felt that the Church was surrendering its ideals to the status quo of society. In time, however, monastic communities themselves often lost their initial idealism and succumbed to the mindset of the current culture. This required a new renewal within monastic life itself to regain the Gospel ideals again. The Middle Ages are marked by a constant pattern of foundation, decline and refoundation in the various forms of monastic life.

Because of their dedication to manual labor and the wise use of resources, monasteries became important centers of social and economic development as well as places of prayer and scholarship. Monasteries, which were originally founded in solitude on the edges of civilization, frequently became the starting point first for market centers and later for towns. As a civilizing force within Western

Europe the men and women of the monastic movement carried forward the vision of Benedict expressed in the "Prologue" of his Rule.

We are therefore now about to institute a school for the service of God, in which we hope nothing harsh nor burdensome will be ordained. But if we proceed in certain things with some little severity, sound reason so advising for the amendment of vices and for the preserving of charity, do not for fear of this forthwith flee from the way of salvation, which is always narrow in the beginning. In living our life, however, and by the growth of faith, when the heart has been enlarged, the path of God's commandments is run with unspeakable loving sweetness; so that never leaving His school, but persevering in the monastery until death in His teaching, we share by our patience in the sufferings of Christ, and so merit to be partakers in His kingdom.

15

Islam

From the end of the fourth century until the early decades of the seventh century, Christianity was the dominant religious movement in the Mediterranean world. Although there was a general framework of Orthodox Catholic Christianity which bound the empire together, the Greek-speaking Christians of the eastern half of the empire and the Latin-speaking Christians of the western half of the empire were confronted with different problems and developed diverse perspectives on the faith and its practice.

Eastern Christianity or the Christianity of the Byzantine empire centered in Constantinople developed within the context of Caesaro-Papism. This theory maintains that the emperor was not only the supreme political authority but also the dominant religious authority in the unified reality of the Christian Roman empire. Until the final collapse of the Byzantine empire in 1453, the life of the Church in all its aspects was under the firm control and direction of the reigning emperor.

The situation was quite different in the western half of the empire. Life in Western Europe underwent a radical change from the mid-fourth century onward because a variety of Germanic peoples moved out of the Rhine valley in Germany and settled in France, Spain, Italy, Britain and North Africa. The Germanic wave of invasion and immigration into the empire by Visigoths, Huns and Vandals was symbolized in 410 when the city of Rome was captured by the Visigoths. Because the Western emperors were weak rulers in the early fifth century and non-existent after 476, the Bishop of Rome became the de facto leader of the western half of the empire. Under the guidance of strong Popes such as Leo the Great (440–461) and Gregory the Great (590–604), the Church in the West sought to preserve the best of classical culture and to bring the Germanic tribes into the mainstream of Catholic Christianity. Into this complex world of Eastern and Western Christianity a new and powerful religious movement, which would radically alter the cultural patterns of the Mediterranean world, emerged from the Arabian desert in the early seventh century—the religion of Islam.

Muhammad

Muhammad was the founder of Islam. The word "Islam" means submission. A Muslim or follower of Muhammad is one who submits to the will of God or Allah.

Muhammad (570–632) was born at Mecca in Arabia of a mercantile family who earned their living as caravan traders. He was a religious leader, an administrator, a warrior and a charismatic prophet. In his lifetime Muhammad built a self-contained religious community with its own laws, government and structure. Today the worldwide Muslim community numbers over five hundred million members.

Muhammad Receiving Revelation from Archangel Gabriel

Seventh century Arabia was an insignificant area on the borders of the Christian Roman empire. Although the native population knew something of the teachings of both Judaism and Christianity, they were pagan animists or syncretists for the most part. At the age of forty, Muhammad had a conversion experience in which he felt himself called to be a prophet who would labor for the salvation of his fellow Arabs. Muslim tradition says that Muhammad received his prophetic call from Allah through the angel Gabriel while engaged in a month-long retreat of prayer and fasting on Mount Hira. The angel Gabriel was to be the normal channel by which Muhammad would receive his revelations from God. The divine revelations, communicated to Muhammad during his lifetime, were committed to writing by his followers and became the holy book of the Muslims, the Koran.

After his conversion experience Muhammad continued to reside in Mecca for the next ten years. During this period he developed Islamic ritual, such as praying five times daily facing Mecca, and a strict ethical code, which, for example, punished a crime such as stealing by cutting off the thief's hand. Religious persecution caused Muhammad and his followers to flee from Mecca to Medina in 622. This flight is known as the hejira and is the date that was later adopted as the first year of the Muslim era. Subsequently, Muhammad raised an army and returned in triumph to Mecca. As a warrior he was enormously successful and his new religious movement began to spread throughout the Near East even during his lifetime.

The Teachings of Islam

Islam emphasized two primary components of religion, which were manifest in the experience of Muhammad himself—the call of God and the response of the human community. For Islam there is only one God, Allah, who is eternal, all-powerful and merciful. Although Allah is totally other, he is also the provident creator of the world who is present in history attending to even the smallest detail in the life of every individual. By reason of their creation and common descent from the first man and woman, all human beings belong to God and are called to respond in obedience to his will for them. In fact, however, the response of the human community to Allah has largely been a history of disobedience. The chief sin of humankind is the sin of idolatry or polytheism, the worship of many gods.

Muslims see human history as the drama of constant tension between faithfulness to the one God and the temptation to polytheism. Throughout history God has sent a series of prophets to call humankind away from polytheism and back to pure and faithful monotheism. Those who heed the call of Allah through the prophets and submit to the divine will go to paradise at the end of their lives; those who do not go to hell when they die. Obedience or submission to Allah's will determined who would go to paradise and who would not.

Although Islam regards Adam as the father of humanity, it does not accept the notion that Adam or his descendants are the image of God. The gulf between the creator and the creature is so great that there is no possibility for human beings to image God. Hence Muslims are violently opposed to any religious image, whether picture or statue, that would try in any way to represent the incomprehensible and totally spiritual reality that is Allah.

The Prophets

The prophets, Noah, Abraham, Moses and Jesus, were each called by Allah to inaugurate a new historical era in which humanity returned to pure monotheism. The major prophetic figures of the Old Testament were common ancestors both to Arabs and Jews. Because Islam does not believe in original sin, there is no need for a savior. Hence for Muhammad Jesus' mission was simply that of another prophet in the line of those called by Allah to restore monotheism. Any interpretation of Jesus' death on the cross as important for human salvation or any understanding of Jesus as God's Son had no place within the teachings of Islam. Muhammad was seen as the last of the prophets, whose mission was to inaugurate the final stage of history, the end time.

Muhammad looked to Abraham as the common ancestor of the Jews and of the Arabs. When his wife Sarah could not initially conceive a child, Abraham took a slave girl named Hagar as a second wife. Hagar bore Abraham a son named Ishmael. Later Sarah also bore Abraham a son called Isaac, who is recognized as one of the great patriarchs of Jewish monotheism. The struggle between Sarah

| 570 | 622, Flight | 632 |
| Muhammad born | to Medina | Muhammad dies |

604
Death of Gregory
the Great

and Hagar over the place of their respective sons led Abraham to abandon Hagar and Ishmael. As they journeyed in the desert wilderness Hagar and Ishmael, according to Islamic tradition, stopped at a place called Mecca. Here the angel Gabriel appeared to them and provided for their needs. Some believe that Hagar and Ishmael were eventually buried at Mecca. The Koran 3:60 states: "Abraham was neither a Jew or a Christian; but he was one of the true religion who submitted to God." As the descendants of Abraham through Hagar and Ishmael, Arabs see themselves and their land of Arabia as having an honored and ancient place in the history of monotheism, which is independent of the Jewish and Christian role in salvation history coming from Isaac and his descendants.

Muhammad understood himself to be a prophet called by Allah to restore pristine Abrahamic monotheism. He was to be the last and greatest of the prophets sent to all the peoples of the world before the end of history. Since Islam was intended to be the new universal religion, Allah dictated his revelation, the scriptures of Islam, to Muhammad through the angel Gabriel. This revelation repeated or dictated by Muhammad to his disciples would become the Koran.

The Five Pillars of Islam

Religious law was not a central concern of the early major religions of the Ancient Near East. Judaism, however, was based upon the Sinai covenant as that was expressed in the law or Torah. In later Judaism, as the Torah developed into the Mishna and finally the Talmud, the law as interpreted by the rabbis in the synagogues became central in Jewish life. While Judaism was based on observance of the law, Christianity was based on the law of love flowing from the Holy Spirit indwelling the hearts of believers.

Islam was similar to Judaism in its preference for external law as a fundamental aspect of its religious faith. Laws for the Islamic community had their origin in the traditions or sayings of Muhammad. As Jewish law sought to explain the obligations flowing from the covenant, so Islamic law concerned the primary obligations of Muslims, known as the "five pillars" of Islam.

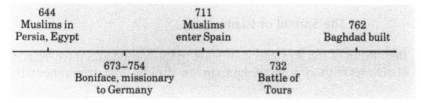

| 644 Muslims in Persia, Egypt | 673–754 Boniface, missionary to Germany | 711 Muslims enter Spain | 732 Battle of Tours | 762 Baghdad built |

The first pillar of Islam is the Muslim profession of faith: "There is no God but Allah and Muhammad is his prophet." Recited with faith before witnesses, this creed or profession of faith confers Islamic identity by making a person a true Muslim. Because Islam has no liturgy, sacramental system or priesthood, this profession of faith is of central significance.

The second pillar of Islam is prayer. Five times daily every Muslim is required to recite a set formula of ritual prayers while bowing in the direction of Mecca. In Arab lands, the people are called to prayer by the muezzin, the prayer leader, who proclaims the times of prayer from the minaret or tower atop the mosque, the Islamic house of prayer. In Islamic tradition, wherever a Muslim places his prayer rug, there is the house of Allah.

The third pillar of Islam is the practice of fasting during the month of Ramadan. The fast was to be a total fast from sunrise to sunset. In Islamic tradition, Muhammad had received his first revelation from the angel Gabriel and his call as a prophet during this month. Hence the fast was seen as a community exercise of repentance and conversion when all submitted themselves again in obedience to the will of Allah.

The fourth pillar of Islam is almsgiving. Muslims were asked to make free will offerings to Allah for the needs of relatives, orphans, travelers and the poor. Donations were also made to assist debtors, slaves, prisoners and those fighting in a holy war.

The fifth and final pillar of Islam is the pilgrimage to Mecca. If possible each Muslim was asked to make a pilgrimage once during life to the holy shrine of the Ka'bah in Mecca. Since the pilgrimage or hajj was the most significant religious event in the life of any Muslim, he or she was expected to abstain from violence, sensuality and luxurious living during the time of the pilgrimage. Wearing a white robe, indicating the special status of a pilgrim, he or she upon arrival in Mecca went to the Ka'bah. This black draped cubal house was believed to contain a stone given to Abraham by the angel Gabriel. The pilgrim walked around the stone seven times, kissing it or touching it at each turn. The hajj gave Muslims a profound sense of the historic and universal character of Islam.

The Spread of Islam

Beginning in the Arabian peninsula in the second and third decades of the seventh century, Islam spread rapidly first throughout the

Near East and then across North Africa and into Spain. The successors to Muhammad as leaders of the Islamic community were called the caliphs. Under the early caliphs, Omar and Ali, the Islamic movement became an empire extending from Spain to India. Later a division occurred among Muhammad's followers over how a caliph was to be chosen. The Sunni Muslims believed that an election was a proper and valid way of choosing a new caliph. The Shiite Muslims, on the other hand, demanded that each new caliph be a direct descendant of the caliph Ali.

In the East, the might of Islam moved against the Byzantine empire and conquered extensive territory until its expansion was checked by the emperor Leo the Isaurian in 717. In the West the forces of Islam crossed North Africa and conquered land as far as Spain. The Muslim advance was finally stopped by Charles Martel at the battle of Tours in 732.

The spread of Islam across a frontier forty-five hundred miles long and a thousand miles deep in the course of one century was truly remarkable. There were several reasons for this. Persians and Byzantines were exhausted fighting each other, and Islam stepped into a void, conquering Syria, Palestine, Persia, Egypt, Cyprus, Rhodes, southern Italy, Sicily, North Africa and Spain. Also, Arabs in battle knew how to use the desert to their advantage. For instance they relied on two animals that made desert travel possible: the Arabian horse whose flaring nostrils take in huge amounts of air and the one-humped camel that can drink twenty-five gallons of water in ten minutes and whose feet compare to balloon tires. The Muslim conquest of the first century remained permanent, with the exception of Spain, Italy and the Mediterranean islands.

Between 750 and 809 the Muslims built the city of Baghdad as the urban center of their new civilization. Their religion often stimulated new artistic and literary development. Everyone had to learn Arabic to read the Koran since it was forbidden to translate "the Book." Thus Arabic came to be the standard written language of the Islamic world.

The caliph Mamun the Great (813–833) built an observatory in Baghdad, founded a university and ordered the great works of Greek scientists and philosophers translated into Arabic. The works of Aristotle and other Greek scientists were available to the Arabs and thus translated. The Arab scholar Avicenna (980–1037) was known for his work on Aristotle and the neo-Platonists which, when later translated into Latin, stimulated European interest.

Muslim scientists adopted Indian numerals, now called Arabic, which included the concept of zero. They began analytical geometry, developed algebra and founded plane and spherical trigonometry. In philosophy the Spanish Muslim Averroes (1126–1198) attempted to wed philosophy with the Koran. His commentaries on Aristotle translated from Arabic into Latin were available to the Christian West by the early thirteenth century.

Thus Muslims came to be the great preservers and transmitters of many works of classical philosophy and science. In the Middle Ages this inheritance passed through Sicily and Spain into the rest of Western Europe.

16

Eastern Christianity

In the year 330 Constantine established the city of Byzantium, later to be called Constantinople, as the capital of the new Christian empire. The transfer of the seat of power from the old Rome to the new Rome of Byzantium was the initial sign of a gradual and unfolding distinction between Western and Eastern Christianity. The death of the emperor Theodosius in 395 signaled the de facto end of a unified Roman empire. Although the empire remained one in theory, the combination of weak emperors in the West and the increasing power and influence of newly arrived immigrant people and their leaders meant the end of real Roman rule by 476. After the fall of Rome in 410 the West went into decline and struggled during the succeeding centuries to maintain some semblance of classical civilization while seeking to convert to Catholic Christianity the immigrant peoples who had invaded the West. During the fifth century the Eastern and Western halves of the Christian Roman empire began to go their separate ways.

Justinian

Under the emperor Justinian (527–565) there was one last attempt to re-establish the unity between the Eastern and Western halves of the empire that had been disrupted by the Germanic invasions. Justinian sent massive military forces into Italy and North Africa in order to destroy the Ostrogothic and Vandal kingdoms. Although these military expeditions were successful, they exhausted the resources of the Byzantine state and destroyed Italy's and Africa's economies. The debilitated local populations and the remaining Byzantine garrisons quickly succumbed to the next wave of Germanic invaders, the Lombards who from 568 onward quickly undid the results of the Byzantine reconquest. Justinian's attempt to revive the empire was also unsuccessful on the Eastern frontiers, where he was unable to stop the Slavic peoples from invading the Balkan peninsula. Amidst his military setbacks in both the West and the East, Justinian did produce a lasting and remarkable accomplishment that witnesses to the sophistication of the Eastern empire, the *Codex Juris Civilis,* the law code of Justinian. The great compilation of Roman law was a gathering of the wisdom of the great jurists of the classical Greco-Roman civilization, the humanizing vision of Christianity and the best insights of Hellenic philosophy.

Justinian conceived the relationship between the empire and the Church as a *symphonia,* a harmonious working together for the common good. The great church in Constantinople, the Hagia Sophia (Holy Wisdom), which had been destroyed by an earthquake, was rebuilt by Justinian in 538 as the symbol of the *symphonia* that should characterize the Christian empire. This masterpiece of Byzantine architecture with its splendid mosaics and marvelous icons of Christ and the saints became the model for all subsequent church buildings throughout the empire in succeeding centuries.

Hagia Sophia

The Eastern Empire: 565–1054

Drastic changes within the Mediterranean world ushered in the Byzantine Middle Ages. By the end of the seventh century, North Africa, Syria, Egypt, Palestine and parts of Italy had been lost to the Muslims or to the Lombards. Similarly invading Slavic peoples had taken control of the Balkans, effectively disrupting overland communication between the East and the West. The Muslim and Slavic threats to what remained of the Byzantine empire meant that the East was unable to assist Italy as it faced the attack of the Lombards. Consequently, the Bishop of Rome, the de facto ruler of Italy, turned for help to the Franks, who as German converts to Catholic Christianity responded to the papal appeal. The papacy and the Franks not only formed an alliance but also created a new vision of the Christian West, symbolized in the coronation of Charlemagne as Holy Roman Emperor on Christmas Day in 800 by Pope Leo III.

From the year 800 on, the Church in the East and the West developed very differently because of varied cultural circumstances. The invasion of the Germanic peoples caused the Church in the West to focus its efforts on preserving what remained of classical culture and trying to convert and civilize the new immigrants within the empire. The Bishop of Rome was the primary coordinator of the efforts of preservation and the dynamic initiator of many missionary endeavors. Because the local clergy were often deficient educationally, the monks became the leaders of cultural and religious development. The monasteries of Western Europe became, in fact, the major centers and the models for Church life in the West. As the various Germanic tribes, who were often Arian Christians when they entered the empire, were gradually assimilated to Catholic Christianity through the missionary efforts of the monks, new possibilities emerged. These opportunities for a more unified Christian West coalesced when Charlemagne was crowned emperor.

Although the East lost a great deal of territory to the Muslims, strong rulers after 717 such as Leo the Isaurian (717–740) stopped the advance of Islam and created the sophisticated medieval Byzantine empire. While the West was becoming a rural and barely literate Church, the East remained an urban Church with an educated clergy and laity. Theological discussion was lively in the Byzantine Church, and missionaries were sent to the newly arrived Slavic peoples in the Balkans.

The experience of Christian life in the East was highly influenced by Caesaro-Papism, the dominance of the Church by the state in the person of the emperor. As the highest authority within the Church, the emperor presided over the government of the Church as that was directed by the four Eastern patriarchs, the bishops of Constantinople, Alexandria, Antioch and Jerusalem. Together with the emperor and the patriarchs, the bishops of the empire gathered in general councils or regional synods and sought to solve the theological and liturgical questions facing the Church.

Between 565 and 1054 the Churches in the East and the West began to feel more and more alienated from one another until finally actual schism or breakdown in ecclesial communion occurred. The causes for the division between the Orthodox East—a Church following the teachings of the early councils and hence called Orthodox— and the Roman West occurred on three levels: the doctrinal, the structural and the ritual.

Doctrinal Controversy

Before the schism or split between Eastern and Western Christianity, the peoples of the two halves of the old empire were already becoming strangers to one another. While the East spoke Greek, the West spoke Latin. Their political experience was also very different. The emperor reigned over a united, if territorially diminished, empire in the East, while the West was struggling to find some unity under Charlemagne and his descendants.

The focus of doctrinal controversy in the ninth century between the Eastern and the Western Churches became the dispute over the *Filioque*. In 381 the second ecumenical council, the First Council of Constantinople, condemned the heretical teaching that the Holy Spirit was a creature unequal to the Father and the Son. The Council declared that the Holy Spirit was of the same divine substance as the Father and the Son and was distinguished from them within the Holy Trinity because he "proceeds from the Father." The Church in the West, however, especially in Spain, as evidenced by the Third Council of Toledo in 589, began to add the words "and the Son" (*Filioque*) to the already established phrase of the Nicene-Constantinopolitan Creed "proceeds from the Father." The Eastern Church refused to recognize that addition because they believed that it was theologically incorrect to say that the Holy Spirit "proceeds from the Father and the Son." The East also felt that it was gravely wrong for one part of the Church to add an element to the creed which had been agreed upon by the whole Church through an ecumenical council.

Underlying the dispute about the *Filioque* were deeper theological questions about the Holy Trinity. Were the Churches disagreeing about the nature of the Christian God? Did they really disagree about the meaning of the procession of the third person of the Trinity? Or is there finally no substantial difference between the two in their understanding of the Holy Spirit? The failure to resolve these questions satisfactorily over the centuries contributed to the split between Eastern Orthodox and Western Catholic Christians.

Structural Differences

A second level of difference between the Eastern and Western approach to Christianity concerned their understanding of political structures as well as Church order or structure. Because of the Germanic invasions, the West experienced a separation from the governmental structures of the Byzantine empire. By crowning Charlemagne as emperor in 800, Pope Leo III established a new political order in the West independent of the Byzantine empire. The Pope

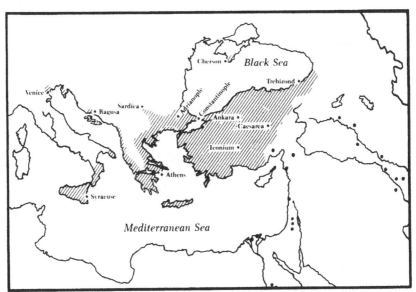

The Byzantine Empire about 814

also gave a new prominence to the papacy in political matters; this was to lead eventually to great struggles between the German emperors and the Popes over the question of ultimate leadership within Western Christendom.

Church order or structures were also conceived differently in the East and the West. The East understood the Church as collegial in nature and held together by the pentarchy, the five patriarchs of the most important Churches of the empire: Rome, Constantinople, Alexandria, Antioch and Jerusalem. Together the five patriarchs were the supreme teachers and judges of all Church matters. The Bishop of Rome held the primacy of honor among the patriarchs because he was the bishop of the city of the apostles Peter and Paul. The other patriarchs also saw themselves as successors to apostolic founders and hence claimed that they had legitimate traditions and rites with which the Bishop of Rome could not interfere.

While the East had four patriarchal sees, the West had only one which claimed apostolic foundation—Rome. The Bishop of Rome developed a form of Church order in the West that was monarchical rather than collegial. Because the Bishop of Rome or the Pope came to exercise political as well as ecclesiastical power in the West, being the only person capable of maintaining order in both the Church and society, his role was very different from that of the Eastern patriarchs. In the East the patriarchs were dependent upon and subservient to the emperor. Because the West had no resident emperor after 476, the Pope came to be more autocratic in both civil and ecclesiastical matters.

The Church in the West came to be more clerical and monastic while the Church in the East made less distinction between the clerical and lay members of the Christian community. Because Eastern Christians placed great emphasis upon tradition and the significance of ecumenical councils, the Church in the East is often called the "Church of the First Seven Ecumenical Councils." The Western Church, while recognizing the importance of the councils, placed more emphasis on the teaching of the Bishop of Rome as the living expression of the authority of the apostle Peter. The conciliarist view of the East stood in marked contrast to the papal view of the West.

Diversity of Spiritual Outlook

Another area of discord between the Churches was the diversity of spiritual outlook symbolized by the West's attitude toward the iconoclastic controversy from 726 to 843. For a series of complex reasons, including the desire to placate the Muslims of Asia Minor, the emperor Leo III (717–740) banned the use of images in churches by his decrees of 726 and 730. Although the Pope supported the veneration of icons and images, many in the West, including some theologians at the court of Charlemagne, misunderstood the viewpoint of the iconodules or supporters of images and seemed to offer support to the iconoclasts or destroyers of images. Much of the difficulty stemmed from the fact that the West misunderstood the meaning of the veneration of images permitted by the Second Council of Nicaea in 787.

In the West statues and holy pictures were considered to be useful symbols in instructing an illiterate society. But the iconodules or supporters of images in the East saw icons or pictures as worthy of veneration because they actually participated, from a neo-Platonic view, in the reality they represented. The iconoclasts and misinformed Westerners thought that the veneration of icons offered by the iconodules bordered on idolatry. In defending the veneration of icons as being in accord with the orthodox faith, the Second Council of Nicaea saw the very reality of the incarnation at stake. For icons, on the level of visible participation in the mysteries of Christ's life and sharing in the holiness of the saints, were made possible because the Incarnate Word had assumed a visible humanity. The East reaffirmed its support of the veneration of icons in 843, but the West's apparent hostility and lack of appreciation for the Byzantine spiritual outlook on icons contributed to the further split between Eastern and Western Christians.

In 1054 legates of the Pope and the Byzantine patriarch Michael Cerularius mutually excommunicated each other at Constantinople over the question of the *Filioque* and papal primacy. Although many subsequent efforts were made to reunite the two Churches, they all finally came to no avail since the theological problems were complicated by numerous political, social and cultural issues as well. Only since the new ecumenical openness occasioned by the Second Vatican Council has there been an increased effort by the Eastern and Western Churches to solve their differences and restore their communion with each other in the one body of Christ.

17

Christian Europe from 600 to 1100

During the early Middle Ages from 600 to 1100 the Church attempted to live the Gospel ideals, to be the people of God and the body of Christ. At the same time the Church was the leading social institution in Western Christian Europe. Christian leaders sought to keep alive the classical heritage of the ancient world while forming the converted Germanic peoples into a new society. The question that faced the Church in this five hundred year period, and the abiding question of every period of history, was the extent to which the Church should adapt itself to the society in which it lived. What is the relationship between Christ and culture, between the Church and secular society? How do individuals and communities find their salvation as they journey to God amidst the realities of the present world?

Pope Gregory I

During the fifth and sixth centuries the Church had to face the demographic changes in Western Europe resulting from the mass migrations of the Germanic peoples. The missionary outreach of the Church was no longer centered in the urban centers of the Greco-

800 Charlemange crowned		910, War opens against Spanish Moslems		1066 Normans conquer England
	843 Iconoclasm ends	909 Cluny founded		1054 Church divides over *filioque*

Roman world as it had been in the first five hundred years of its existence. The new mission of the Christian community now turned to converting and forming peoples whose culture was rural and barely literate. The guiding force of this cultural transformation in the West was the papacy, assisted by the dedicated efforts of the monks.

Gregory the Great (590–604) exemplifies the difficult tasks that faced the Bishops of Rome during the late empire and the early Middle Ages. The Popes had to deal with the Byzantine emperors in the East; they had to maintain the life of the Church in the surviving urban centers of the West and they had to organize missionary expeditions to the Germanic tribes now settled in northern Europe. Born in a noble Roman family around 540, Gregory became a monk in 574 after a period of public service that included acting as prefect of the city of Rome. The needs of the Church, however, called Gregory from the silence of the monastic life to the important position of papal representative at the court of the Eastern emperor in Byzantium. After serving seven years in this post, Gregory returned to his monastery in Rome. Once more, however, the needs of the Church required the holiness and the administrative genius of Gregory. He was elected Pope in 590.

Because of his experience in Byzantium, Gregory was convinced that the future of the Western Church was to be found in tapping the energies of the newly arrived Germanic peoples rather than in struggling to recapture a faded past with the Eastern empire. Turning his efforts and attention to the Germanic peoples, Gregory sent missionaries to France and England. His efforts, especially in England, met with great success. The monastic ideals carried by the first Roman missionaries to England were enthusiastically received by the new converts. Within a hundred years Anglo-Saxon missionaries from the British Isles, such as Boniface, who later was the patron saint of Germany, returned to the mainland of Europe. They became an integral part of the vast missionary movement launched by Gregory and continued by his successors. Anglo-Saxon missionaries forged strong links between the Germanic peoples of northern Europe and the Bishops of Rome.

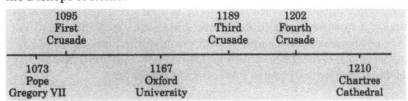

1095		1189	1202	
First		Third	Fourth	
Crusade		Crusade	Crusade	

1073	1167		1210
Pope	Oxford		Chartres
Gregory VII	University		Cathedral

The Papacy and the Carolingians

The links between the Germanic peoples and the papacy became profoundly important in the mid-eighth century. Threatened by the Lombards, the last of the Germanic peoples to arrive in Italy as adherents of the Arian heresy, Pope Stephen II (752–757) appealed for help to Pepin, the leader of the Frankish royal family known as the Carolingians. Traveling to what is now northern France, Stephen made it clear to the Catholic ruler, Pepin, that the Lombards had stolen territories belonging to the Church. Pepin forced the Lombards to return the captured lands and conferred additional territory in central Italy upon the papacy. This area, first known as the patrimony of St. Peter, became the basis for the Papal States which existed until the unification of Italy in 1870. In a period of history when land ownership was the basis of power and authority, the Popes used the patrimony of St. Peter as a way of securing the Church's freedom in an increasingly complex feudal society.

The coronation of Charlemagne, the greatest of the Carolingian rulers, as Holy Roman Emperor by Pope Leo III in 800 both strengthened and strained the bonds between the Germanic peoples and the papacy. The fortunes of the Carolingians and the Bishops of Rome were now linked together in a common concern about the Church and society in Western Europe. These shared concerns, however, left unresolved the question of whether the Holy Roman Emperor or the Roman Pope was finally the ultimate authority in Western Christendom. Medieval society would expend considerable time and energy in trying to answer that question.

Feudal Europe

Feudalism was the economic and social system which determined the basic life patterns of early medieval Europe. The basis of feudalism was land ownership. A land owner or lord conferred a grant of land (*feudum*) upon one of his subjects, a vassal, on the condition of receiving certain services such as military assistance. In this mutually advantageous private contract, the lord received loyalty and support in overseeing and defending his lands while the vassal received economic security and military protection. Subject to the vassals were the serfs or peasants who farmed the land and cared for the needs of the estate in return for food and protection.

The Church in general and monasteries in particular were also deeply involved in the feudal system. As land owners, bishops and abbots were feudal lords who in turn had vassals and great manors cared for by serfs. Because Germanic peoples conceived the king as the chief land owner of the kingdom, all property, including Church property, was at his disposal. The process whereby the king as a lay lord conferred a diocese or an abbey upon a bishop or an abbot as his vassal is known as lay investiture, i.e., the conferral of the ecclesiastical office, symbolized by the land which belonged to it, by a lay ruler. Because the practice of lay investiture gave power and authority over Church leaders to civil rulers, it came to be seen as an abuse which threatened the freedom of the Church and its mission to speak out when necessary against unjust rulers.

Two further problems besides lay investiture which confronted the Church in the early Middle Ages were simony and concubinage. Simony meant that Church offices, such as those of bishop and abbot, were given by lay lords to churchmen in exchange for land or money; concubinage meant that bishops and priests were not observing the law of celibacy but were living with women as if they were married to them. These serious violations of Church discipline necessitated a reform or renewal that would restore the balanced tension between the Church as human institution with sinful members and the Church as mystery with men and women living lives of Gospel holiness and service.

The Reform of Cluny

The reform of the early medieval Church began in 909 when Duke William of Aquitaine deeded over a piece of land at Cluny in southeastern France to the holy abbot Berno. During the reign of Charlemagne's successors (814–887) the rule of Benedict became normative for Western monasticism. Monasteries grew and prospered, becoming important cultural and educational institutions as well as spiritual centers. However, the monasteries also became deeply involved in the feudal system and experienced a loss of spiritual fervor because of lay investiture, simony and concubinage. Duke William and Abbot Berno founded Cluny to be a center of reform that would renew early medieval society. Key to that reform was the decision that the monastery of Cluny would stand outside of the feudal system by being independent of local lords and bishops and subject directly to the Pope.

Cluny around 1157

Six abbots ruled Cluny for a period of two hundred years (909–1109), providing the strong leadership that was necessary to implement continually the original purpose of the foundation. Cluny attempted to give new meaning to the Rule of St. Benedict by returning to a life of prayer, obedience and simplicity. The Benedictine idea of the monastery as a family eventually became the basis for establishing a federation of over one thousand monasteries, independent of feudal structures, that were guided by the abbot of Cluny and the Bishop of Rome. The spiritual renewal begun at Cluny quickly spread to other parts of the Church, since Cluniac monks were often chosen for important positions of leadership as bishops and ultimately Popes. The Cluniac reform would lead to the Gregorian reform, named after the monk Pope Gregory VII. The Gregorian reform was a vast movement of moral, disciplinary and administrative renewal which affected not only the Church but the whole of early medieval society.

The Gregorian Reform

During the tenth and eleventh centuries, the German Ottonian emperors and certain Roman families struggled with each other for control of the papacy. Emperor Otto I (936–973) treated the universal Church as though it were the feudal Church of Germany. The lay investiture of bishops and abbots in Germany by the emperor now became the model for dealing with the Bishops of Rome. Seeking to remove the papacy from the control of feuding Italian families, the German emperors began appointing men of their own choosing to the office of Bishop of Rome. Such was the situation in the mid-eleventh century when one of the Popes appointed by Emperor Henry III (1039–1056), Pope Leo IX (1049–1054), embraced the principles of the Cluniac reform and set the Church on the road to freedom from imperial control.

In 1073 one of Leo IX's chief supporters, the monk Hildebrand, was chosen as Pope, without imperial interference, and took the name Gregory VII. For over twenty years Gregory had been secretary to five Popes and understood the great need for a general reform and renewal within the Church. He believed in the necessity of a strong and independent Church ruled by the Pope and the bishops under his direction.

Gregory understood the whole Church as a monastery with the Pope as its abbot. All members of the Church, including the emperor, were to be charitable to one another and obedient to the Pope as their common father. United under the papacy, the whole of Christendom would move harmoniously on its journey through this world to the full happiness of the kingdom of heaven. Although Gregory understood that the temporal and spiritual orders were distinct in principle, he maintained that in the actual order of things the temporal needed to be subject to the spiritual for the sake of the common good.

In continuity with his predecessors, Pope Leo I (440–461) and Pope Gregory I (590–604), Gregory VII reaffirmed the importance of a strong papacy within the life of the Church and reasserted papal primacy over against the claims of the German emperors. Wanting to free the Church from the problems and moral decay associated with lay investiture, simony and concubinage, Gregory took strong action against laymen and clerics involved in such practices. He sought to appoint worthy and holy men to all the offices of leadership within the Church. The new model for the life of the clergy was the monastic outlook of dedication to prayer, work and the pastoral ministry by men who were celibate, obedient and poor insofar as possible. The Church that moved from the early Middle Ages to the high Middle Ages of the twelfth and thirteenth centuries was a community renewed by reform and ready to embark on its future with confidence and renewed commitment to the Gospel.

FOR FURTHER READING

Peter Brown, *Augustine of Hippo* (Berkeley and Los Angeles: University of California Press, 1969).

Peter Brown, *The World of Late Antiquity A.D. 150–750* (London: Harcourt Brace Jovanovich, Inc., 1971). This book offers an excellent overview of the Byzantine Empire and the rise of Islam.

David Knowles, *Christian Monasticism* (New York: McGraw-Hill Book Company, 1969).

C. H. Lawrence, *Medieval Monasticism* (London and New York: Longman, 1984). This book provides a broad understanding of the development of Western monasticism from the time of St. Benedict to the thirteenth century.

18

The Medieval Catholic Experience

Religion is a lived experience that expresses itself within a specific culture. During the high Middle Ages, the twelfth and thirteenth centuries, the Christianity of Western Europe expressed itself in five metaphors that symbolized the medieval Catholic experience: the monk, the pilgrim, the knight, the scholar and the cathedral.

The Monk

Medieval monasticism centered on the various branches of the Benedictine family. In the early Middle Ages, the Benedictine monastery of Cluny and the many monasteries associated with the Cluniac movement contributed to the general renewal of the Church and played a significant role in the Gregorian reform. When Cluny began to decline and lose its vision of reform in the early twelfth century, a very strict branch of the Benedictines, the Cistercians from Citeaux in southeastern France, emerged as a new force of renewal. The most famous Cistercian and the person who best symbolized the monk within the medieval Catholic experience was Bernard of Clairvaux.

Bernard was born in 1090 and joined the Cistercians in 1112. Three years later he became the founding abbot of Clairvaux, where he ruled for thirty-eight years. At the time of Bernard's death in 1153, Clairvaux had established sixty-eight other monasteries. By their strict observance of the Rule of St. Benedict, the Cistercians promoted prayer, work, silence and simplicity. Bernard was a preacher, an organizer, an administrator, a writer and a mystic. He believed strongly in the Christian ideals of service and sacrifice and deeply influenced a number of Christian leaders, especially his former student, Pope Eugene III (1145–1153).

Bernard made a great contribution to medieval Catholic life by his spiritual writings. He believed that the goal of Christian life was an experiential awareness of God's presence and God's love through prayer. Because he feared that philosophical speculation could lead to pride, Bernard taught that love of God and one's neighbor far exceeded the value of learned tomes and philosophical discussion. The supreme manifestation of divine and human love was the mystery of the incarnation. In assuming the fleshly reality of the material world, the Word of God fully entered into human history in Jesus Christ. Bernard taught that Christians should meditate on the life, death and resurrection of Jesus in order to understand God's love for them and how they should love one another. The Christocentric and affective theology of the abbot of Clairvaux also emphasized the role of Mary in the life of the Church and in the lives of individual Christians. Bernard's Marian piety reflects the increasing significance of the Virgin in Western spirituality that one finds reflected in the art and sculpture of the Romanesque cathedrals of the early twelfth century.

The Pilgrim

A pilgrimage is a religiously motivated journey to a sacred shrine or holy place. The medieval pilgrimage became a metaphor for the journey of the human person searching for salvation and eternal life with God in the next world while traveling through this world.

Pilgrimage is a phenomenon found in all religions. Sometimes the motive for a pilgrimage is the desire for a cure from some illness or the need for spiritual assistance. At other times the motive for a pilgrimage represents the fulfillment of a vow or an act of thanksgiving for some favor or gift that has been received. Christian pilgrimages emerged during the first seven centuries of the Church's life and were originally journeys to the places within the Holy Land rendered significant by some event in the life of Christ, such as the Holy Sepulcher, the place of Christ's entombment and resurrection in Jerusalem.

Later, monasteries associated with the hermits and monks of the desert became places of pilgrimage. In the late fourth century Pope Damasus (366–384) restored the catacombs, the underground burial places of the early Roman Christians. Subsequently Rome in general and the tombs of Peter and Paul in particular came to be major sites of pilgrimage in the Christian world. Besides Jerusalem and Rome, Compostela in Spain, the burial place of the apostle James the Greater, and Canterbury in England, the site of the martyrdom of Thomas à Becket, were favorite destinations for medieval pilgrims.

A pilgrimage involved many rituals and specific patterns of behavior. Before setting out on the journey, the pilgrims would put their affairs in order and obtain written authorization from the parish priest. Wearing special identifiable dress that usually included a hat and a walking staff, the pilgrim received a special liturgical blessing that asked for protection on the journey that was being undertaken. Along the great pilgrimage routes there were a series of hostels established by the Church to provide accommodations and protection for pilgrims. When they arrived at the shrine or holy place, they usually received the sacraments of penance and the Holy Eucharist. Hoping for some cure, pilgrims often spent whole nights in prayer at the tomb of the saint. If their prayers were answered, pilgrims usually left behind crutches or models of some part of the body that had been cured as symbols of gratitude to God who had extended mercy to them through the saint's intercession.

A pilgrimage was both an exterior geographical journey and an interior spiritual journey. Through contact with the spiritual realities of the Christian religion on a new level, pilgrims hoped to deepen their own sense of the holy and the meaning of faith. The experience of pilgrimage was a liberation from profane social structures and the beginning of a new commitment to the Christian faith.

Medieval Catholic pilgrimages had a bonding effect on the whole social structure of Christendom since the pilgrim moved into the larger social community and experienced a new sense of universalism. Like art and liturgy, pilgrimages contributed to a sense of oneness amidst diversity. Pilgrimages also became occasions for the exchange of news and the diffusion of new ideas.

The Knight

The experience of knights fighting in the crusades was also an important dimension of medieval Catholic life. A crusade was a medieval military expedition organized by the Church for the liberation of the Holy Land and the defense of the Christian faith. In 1074 Pope Gregory VII (the monk Hildebrand) called for a crusade against the

Muslims in Palestine who were harassing the Eastern Empire and persecuting Western pilgrims. However, Gregory's struggle with Henry IV of Germany over the question of lay investiture prevented the crusade from ever becoming a reality.

The Byzantine emperor Alexius I (1081–1118) appealed to Pope Urban II (1088–1099) for assistance in defending the Eastern empire against the forces of Islam. Desiring reunion with the Eastern Church and also desiring to help set free the holy places in Palestine, Pope Urban called for the first crusade in 1095. While the primary motive for going into battle against the Seljuk Turks, who had replaced the Arabs as rulers of Palestine, was religious, there were certainly political, economic and social factors present as well.

Pope Urban's call for a great crusade to liberate the holy places met with great popular enthusiasm and assumed the form of a massive pilgrimage to Palestine. The first response, among the estimated number of nearly a million people who had some part in the crusade movement, came from thousands of peasants who marched from Western Europe to the East through Hungary and the Balkans under the leadership of Peter the Hermit and Walter the Penniless. Many of these unfortunate people died on route and the rest were easy targets for the soldiers of Islam. The unorganized peasants' crusade was followed by the first crusade (1096–1099), under the leadership of outstanding French nobles, such as Godfrey of Bouillon and Raymond of Toulouse. This highly organized military effort successfully captured Jerusalem in 1099. To maintain control over the holy places and to protect and serve pilgrims, two military orders, i.e., groups of knights who also took monastic vows, the Knights Templars and the Knights Hospitalers, came into existence.

In 1146 Bernard of Clairvaux preached the second crusade (1147–1149). Although this expedition to the Holy Land was led by the German emperor Conrad III (1138–1152) and the king of France, Louis VII (1137–1180), it was a disastrous failure for Western Christendom. In 1187 at Hattin, in Palestine, the great Muslim leader Saladin defeated the crusaders living in the Holy Land and captured Jerusalem.

The third crusade (1189–1192) was led by the three greatest rulers of Western Europe, the German emperor Frederick Barbarossa (1152–1190), the king of France, Philip Augustus (1180–1223), and the king of England, Richard the Lionhearted (1189–1199). Because the rulers quarreled among themselves, little was accomplished except gaining free access to Jerusalem for pilgrims.

The fourth crusade (1202–1204), initiated by Pope Innocent III

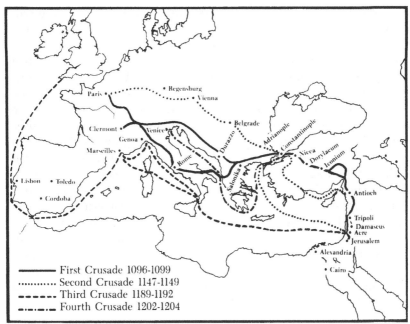

First Crusade 1096-1099
Second Crusade 1147-1149
Third Crusade 1189-1192
Fourth Crusade 1202-1204

Routes of the Crusading Armies

(1198–1216), was diverted by the Venetians to Constantinople. Although the West gained political control of Constantinople, once more placing the Eastern Church under the authority of the Pope, the atrocities committed by the crusaders against Eastern Christians created a formidable barrier to reconciliation between the Greek and Latin Churches. The fifth (1218–1221), sixth (1228–1229), seventh (1248–1250) and eighth (1270) crusades launched throughout the rest of the thirteenth century had very few positive results. The fall of the crusader citadel at Acre to the Muslims in 1291 marked the end of effective military action by Western Christian knights in the Holy Land.

Although many knights went on crusades for the wrong reasons and committed acts of atrocity contrary to the teachings of Christianity, for others a crusade was the occasion for a deeper conversion and an opportunity to do penance for previous sin. Recognizing the sincerity of the knights, the Church granted to crusaders a plenary indulgence or full remission of the temporal punishment due to sin.

The crusades produced varied results within the overall framework of medieval society. They stimulated the development of pilgrimages to the Holy Land and contributed to the notion of chivalry as an ideal for the Christian knight. Initially the calling of the crusades enhanced papal prestige and served as a bonding force across national and ethnic boundaries. The fourth crusade, however, damaged papal credibility and contributed to the enduring antagonism that had been developing between Eastern and Western Christians.

On the economic level the crusades increased contact with the Orient and acted as a stimulus to trade. Italian cities such as Venice and Genoa became thriving centers of commerce as new trade routes to the East and the desire for Oriental goods grew. Although the crusaders transferred their feudal structures to the lands conquered in the Middle East, at home in Western Europe the crusades contributed to the weakening of feudalism. Knights often left their lands and manors without adequate supervision and protection. Serfs frequently used the absence of the lord of the manor as an opportunity to leave the land and look for a better life in the burgeoning cities of the twelfth and thirteenth centuries. Although the crusades profoundly influenced the development of the idea of "knight" as a Christian ideal, the actual experience of many medieval Christians also brought that ideal into serious question.

The Scholar

Scholasticism (1050–1350) was an intellectual movement that was profoundly formative for medieval Catholic experience. The term "scholasticism" is derived from the Greek word "schole," i.e., the place where learning occurs. Scholasticism is the attempt to use reason in trying to understand the truths of faith by correlating philosophical views with biblical views. It was first applied to the teachers in Charlemagne's court and then extended to medieval scholars who were attempting to use philosophy as an aid to theology. The developing scholasticism of the monastic and cathedral schools of the twelfth century reached its full flowering in the great universities of the thirteenth century.

A significant factor in the development of medieval scholasticism was the reintroduction of Aristotle's work into the Christian West. Famous Arab scholars such as Averroes (1126–1198) and Jewish scholars like Moses Maimonides (1135–1204) in Spain had translated the works of Aristotle from Greek to Arabic. Channeled through Spain and Sicily, the works of these Arab and Jewish scholars were in turn translated into Latin. Between 1140 and 1260 all the works of Aristotle once more became part of the intellectual and cultural environment of the Christian world.

The scholars of this period tried to use the philosophical tools provided by Aristotle to organize the truths of faith and to show the harmony between reason and revelation. The question asked by the scholars was: "How can we use reason to understand the faith better?"

One of the early fathers of scholasticism was Anselm (1033–1109), who later became archbishop of Canterbury. Anselm represents a different stance toward the intellectual life than that represented by Bernard. For Bernard philosophy was not really important or significant since the personal experience of God in prayer, not reason, was the foundation for theology. Anselm did not deny the role of prayer in the life of the theologian, but he still believed that reasoning and philosophy could contribute to an understanding of the faith. In his work called the *Proslogion,* Anselm offers his famous ontological argument for the existence of God: everyone has an idea of a perfect Supreme Being. Such a Being must possess existence since lack of existence would be an imperfection and thus contradictory to the idea of a Supreme Being. What exists in reality is a greater perfection than what exists only in the mind. Therefore, God exists.

In his work the *Monologion,* Anselm offers a cosmological argument for the existence of God: human beings have many goods in this life. These goods are reflections of a Supreme Good through which all good exists. But an infinite regression is impossible. Therefore, the cause of all good is God.

In his work called *Cur Deus Homo? (Why Did God Become Man?),* Anselm presented his theory of the atonement by explaining how human beings are reconciled to God through Christ. Since human sin was an infinite offense against God, the debt owed to God because of sin was also infinite. Only one who was both divine and human could pay such a debt. Therefore it is the death of Christ, the God-Man, on the cross, as an infinite sacrifice, that pays the debt of sin and reconciles human beings to God. As the Middle Ages saw Bernard as the perfect exemplar of the monk, so Anselm was seen as the perfect model for the Christian scholar.

The Cathedral

The four metaphors discussed thus far as symbols of the medieval Catholic experience have been persons: the monk, the pilgrim, the

knight and the scholar. The final metaphor, which most fully represents the flowering of medieval Catholicism, is the cathedral.

The ethos of Catholicism has always been sacramental. Precisely
because of the incarnation, i.e., God becoming one with humanity,
the Catholic vision embraced all created reality. It was a fundamental Catholic belief that persons, nature and objects could image God
and spiritual reality. In fact, it was through creation, as sacramental or symbolic, that one arrived at the experience of God.

In the first three centuries of the Church's existence, Christians
came together in small groups, meeting in private homes to celebrate the Eucharist. In these house churches the Christian communities experienced the shared life and hope that gave them the
strength to survive in the often hostile environment of the pagan
Roman world. The phenomenal growth of Christianity after the
Rescript of Toleration in 313 made these house churches inadequate
to meet the needs of the Church as it became the state religion of the
empire.

Since Christian worship was now public worship, the Church
chose the most common form of Roman public buildings, the basilica, as the locus for its liturgical life. The basilica was a large assembly hall which could accommodate a sizable number of people. The
layout of the basilica highlighted the understanding of the Church
and its ministry prevalent at that time. Thus the bishop and the
clergy occupied one end of the large nave, the apse, and sat on a
slightly raised platform facing the congregation. The place of the
laity was the nave or main body of the church. The believers were
seen as recipients of the instruction and sacramental ministrations
of the clergy. The chair from which the bishop preached and presided
was called the "cathedra." The church where the bishop officially
had his chair or place of teaching came to be called the cathedral. As
Christianity moved out of the cities of the Roman empire and into
the rural areas of Western Europe, the early missionaries established new churches and invited the local artists to decorate those
churches in accord with their own understanding of Christianity.

From the fifth to the tenth centuries, church building occurred
throughout Western Europe. These early medieval churches were
often very small and showed very little architectural or artistic sophistication due to the social and political upheaval caused by the
Germanic invasions and the breakdown of law and order in the
Western half of the empire. Whether they were ancient basilicas in
the remaining cities of the empire or small country parishes, these
church buildings provided the sacramental context in which the

Christian communities of the West celebrated and nourished their faith in the expectation of better days ahead.

The tenth and eleventh centuries saw the development of Cluny and the Gregorian reform. Both of these interrelated religious movements provided the stimulus for a springtime of creativity. Architects and artists began constructing and decorating new churches in all parts of Europe. The magnificent churches and cathedrals built between 1000 and 1400 were a remarkable achievement that required enormous human effort. They stand as monuments to the communal experience of medieval Catholicism and as expressions of commitment and spiritual vision.

Romanesque

Romanesque architecture was an imitation of ancient Roman architecture with adaptations necessary for the changed circumstances and the different needs of the medieval world. The walls of Romanesque churches were often very thick, with small openings for light. The fortress character of Romanesque churches provided security in the still turbulent society of the tenth and eleventh centuries and symbolized the strength of the Church in the face of all the forces of violence and evil.

Romanesque churches and cathedrals were often the sites of famous shrines which housed important relics of the saints. Hence these churches needed to be able to accommodate large numbers of pilgrims gathered for the Eucharist in the nave of the church as well as provide for the needs of smaller groups. Thus besides the main altar in the nave, there were altars in chapels along the walls of the church where small groups of pilgrims could celebrate the Eucharist. Since the relics of the church were often kept in a shrine behind the main altar or in a crypt underneath the church, Romanesque churches had large aisles or ambulatories which enabled pilgrims to move around the church and to have access to the shrine even when the Eucharist was being celebrated in the main body of the church.

The private or small group Masses celebrated in the side chapels indicated a shift in liturgical understanding. In the early Christian period the Eucharist was understood as the communal celebration of the Lord's Supper by the whole people of God. In the Middle Ages the Eucharist became a clerical act of worship, which was offered by the priests for the particular intentions of specific individuals among the faithful.

The Gothic Style *(Notre Dame de Paris)*

Gothic

In the twelfth and thirteenth centuries Romanesque architecture yielded to Gothic architecture, a new form developed first in northern France. Gothic churches and cathedrals had high thin walls which were filled with stained glass thus making the interior of the church a sea of light. High ceilings with ribbed vaulting and the use of flying buttresses or exterior supporting arches allowed for the weight of the ceiling to be distributed to various areas of the building. Every line of a Gothic cathedral seems to be vertical with an upward thrust that beckons the believer into the mystery of God beyond all understanding. The experience of the light-filled interior seems to transform reality and symbolize creation itself as already sharing in the radiance of God. The Gothic cathedral was the visual symbol of the medieval Catholic experience that saw life as the ascending light-filled journey to God which ended in the beatific vision of heaven.

19

The Friar Movement

Thirteenth Century Europe

Western Europe underwent rapid social change in the thirteenth century. Feudalism, which had been the fundamental political structure for several centuries, began to yield to the larger political realities of the nation-states. A new urban economy began to replace the feudal agricultural economy. The emerging towns and cities developed a distinct merchant class, which formed trade guilds that were often competitive and monopolistic. Between the old classes of the nobles and the serfs, a new middle class appeared composed of the prosperous merchants in the towns and cities.

The thirteenth century Church experienced the on-going phenomenon of the tension between the charismatic or Spirit-filled and the institutional dimensions of the Church. From the perspective of the Christian faith, the Church as a community of believers is always a mystery. It is simultaneously both the presence of the risen Christ in his community through the power of the Holy Spirit and a visibly structured institution within society. During the thirteenth century a number of strong Popes such as Innocent III (1198–1216) and Innocent IV (1243–1254) sought to strengthen the internal and external aspects of the Church as an institution within medieval society. At the same time various lay groups, such as the Waldensians, adopted a counter-cultural way of living Christian life. Emphasizing poverty and the preaching of the Gospel as primary elements of Christian life, they espoused a vision of the Church that was anti-institutional and anti-clerical. In their call for renewal, however, they succumbed to the temptation of elitism, of forming a Church only for the pure and the sinless.

In southern France, the Albigenses, a modern form of Manichaeanism, taught that matter in general and the body in particular were evil and caused by an evil principle. This dualist heresy, which had its origin in the teachings of the Persian religious thinker Mani (216–276), had come to Western Europe from Bulgaria via the medieval trade routes in the eleventh and twelfth centuries. The Albigenses (the name derives from the city of Albi near Toulouse) offered a viable religious alternative for many men and women who were alienated from the institutional Church.

There had been many movements of renewal within the Catholic Church during the eleventh and twelfth centuries. Cluny represented an attempt to recapture the original spirit of St. Benedict. The Cistercian movement, under the leadership of Bernard of Clairvaux, deepened and went beyond the Cluniac reform. The object of both these renewal movements was the renovation of monasticism, which existed primarily for the salvation of the individual. It was believed that one would be reborn through a routine of prayer, manual labor and community life.

Monasticism offered a model for living that few in the world could follow. Hence there was a thirst among the ordinary men and women believers for another model of Christian piety that would address the religious needs of the laity. Similarly the Church needed to respond to the urban society that was emerging all over Europe. The spiritual vitality of the thirteenth century shifted from the monastic life to the apostolic life in the friar movement. The Church's response to the needs and signs of the times was the creation of a group of apostolic religious—the friars—who would minister to the urban population and especially those who had been educated in the new universities as doctors and lawyers.

The Friars

One can understand the friars better by contrasting their ideals and outlook with those of the monks. Both monks and friars sought to imitate Christ, but the monk followed the path of the contemplative Christ while the friar chose the apostolic life as described in the Gospels. Monks were concerned with their own conversion and spiritual rebirth; hence in their desire for silence and solitude they built

		1204 Crusaders sack Constantinople		1206 Genghis Khan		1215 Magna Carta	
1170 Dominic born	1182 Francis born					1225 Aquinas born	

their monasteries at the edges of civilization and on rural frontiers. Their life was a routine of prayer and work (*ora et labora*) with an emphasis on obedience, penance and especially stability. The latter meant that monks would live always in the same monastery. The friars, following the apostolic Christ, sought to be of service to the Church at large by working for the conversion of others. Thus they built their religious houses (priories and friaries) in towns and cities where they were mobile and free of encumbrances. Taking the Gospel to the new urban and university centers, they sought their own conversion and sanctity in apostolic work. The Dominicans, the Franciscans, the Carmelites and the Augustinians were all groups of friars established in the thirteenth century.

Dominicans

The Dominicans were founded by Dominic Guzman (1170–1221), a man dedicated to following Christ the preacher. Dominic founded an Order of Preachers who embraced poverty as a sign of credibility and as a way of freedom that allowed the friars to go anywhere to preach the Gospel. Dominic also believed that in order to preach the Gospel effectively it was necessary to study; hence the Dominicans moved into the developing university system at the very beginning of their history. In fact, study replaced manual labor in the life of the Dominican friar. The Order of Preachers was dedicated to the praise of God, to knowing about God and to preaching the Gospel of Jesus Christ in any possible situation.

Franciscans

The Order of Friars Minor or Franciscans was founded by Francis of Assisi (1182–1226). Like the Dominicans they imitated Christ by following the apostolic way, but Francis chose Christ the poor man as the model for his life. Francis was not a priest and most of the early Franciscans were laymen. They sought to be humble witnesses and itinerant preachers, giving example by their poverty. Franciscans were at the service of the urban poor and preached the need for conversion and penance. The simplicity and joy of Francis and his

	1275	1300
1265	Marco Polo	Aztec confederacy
Dante born	in China	in Mexico

1260
*Summa
Theologica*

Francis of Assisi *(after Giotto)*

first followers counteracted the example of heretical lay groups outside the Church such as the Waldensians. The Franciscans offered
the laity a spirituality which was filled with joy, concern for others,
respect for nature and Gospel simplicity.

The Friars and Society

Both monks and friars attempted to meet the spiritual needs of
medieval society by responding to the call of the Spirit and the signs

of the times in a Gospel context. Each form of religious life asked how to encounter Christ on the journey to salvation and how best to serve the Christian community. The emphasis of each, however, was slightly different.

The monastic outlook was greatly influenced by the Augustinian world view which saw the human person as a sinner engaged in a journey of healing toward salvation. The outlook of the friars, based on St. Bernard, was more optimistic about the human situation and the potential for doing good. The human Christ, who redeemed humankind out of love, became the model for Christian living. As Romanesque churches signified the monastic outlook, so Gothic churches with their light and peace symbolized the spirit of the friars. The city of man in the thirteenth century was the new urban society emerging throughout Western Europe. The friar movement aided the Church in this new environment by responding to the challenge to preach the Gospel in this new context.

20

Thomas Aquinas—
A New World View

The Life of Thomas

Thomas Aquinas was born around 1225 at Roccasecca near Naples in Italy, the youngest son of Count Landulf of Aquino, a relative of the emperor Frederick. His family sent him as a young boy to study under the Benedictines. They envisioned a distinguished ecclesiastical career for Thomas, planning that he would become abbot of the great monastery of Monte Cassino.

While studying at the University of Naples, however, Thomas, at the age of nineteen, decided to enter the recently established Dominican Order. Overcoming the fierce opposition of his family who were totally against this decision, he completed his novitiate as a Friar Preacher and went to study under the famous Dominican doctor, Albert the Great, first at Paris and then at Cologne. It was under Albert that Thomas first came in contact with an organized presentation of the philosophy of Aristotle. Later Aquinas returned to the University of Paris where he finished his theological studies and began his teaching career.

Thomas spent his life primarily as a professor and a writer, teaching at the University of Paris and various Dominican schools, as well as at the papal court in Viterbo and Orvieto. Aquinas commented in writing on the various books of the Old and New Testament as well as on the works of Aristotle such as *Physics, Metaphysics* and *Ethics*. Among the more than one hundred different books which he authored, Thomas' two most famous works were the *Summa Theologica* and the *Summa Contra Gentiles*.

During his lifetime Aquinas was embroiled in various theological and philosophical controversies. At Paris he disputed with more conservative Augustinian theologians, like the Franciscan Bonaventure, as well as radical Aristotelians, like Siger of Brabant. He also had to defend himself and other friars against the attacks of secular clerics who opposed the presence of Dominicans and Franciscans on the theological faculty of the University of Paris.

Constantly on the move, visiting the great intellectual centers of Europe, Thomas lived a busy life of preaching, teaching and writing. At the age of forty-eight on December 6, 1273, he underwent a profound spiritual experience. As a result of this he wrote: "I cannot go on. . . . All that I have written seems to me like so much straw compared to what I have seen and what has been revealed to me." He did not write or teach after this and died three months later on March 7, 1274.

In 1277 Stephen Tempier, the bishop of Paris, condemned certain doctrines being taught by theologians at the University of Paris. The censure was an implicit condemnation of some teachings of Thomas. On July 18, 1323, less than fifty years later, Pope John XXII (1316–1334) officially canonized Aquinas, and the implicit condemnation of his teaching was revoked in 1325. Thomas was declared a "doctor" of the Church in 1567, and over the centuries his teaching became increasingly influential. In 1879 Pope Leo XIII (1878–1903) enjoined the study of Aquinas in all Catholic seminaries and universities.

Aquinas was a genius and a saint who offered the Catholic world a view which to some degree replaced the perspective of Augustine. While Augustine's world view held sway for almost one thousand years, from 450 to 1400, Aquinas' view has predominated from then until the present.

Thomas as Friar Preacher

Thomas Aquinas was born in the age of the friar movement which sought to imitate Christ in his apostolic or missionary life. Friars were concerned with proclaiming the message of the Gospel to people living in the newly developed towns and cities. Deeply committed to a life of poverty in imitation of Christ, the friars were a free and mobile group of apostles, unencumbered by the possession of material goods. Because the Dominicans in particular saw study as essential to their mission to preach the word of God, they made the university environment synonymous with the Dominican charism.

Aquinas was a product of his time and culture. Although he had great natural ability, the dynamism and opportunities offered by the friar movement provided the occasion for the outstanding development of his native talents. Thomas joined the Dominicans because the order's emphasis on study and intellectual development matched his own inclinations. The Dominican ideal of searching for, discovering and disseminating the truth found a deep resonance in the mind and heart of Aquinas. He found a true home in the Dominican environment and contributed greatly to the preaching and teaching mission of the order as he studied and grew intellectually in his vocation as a friar preacher.

Thomas and the University

Universities were organized guilds of masters and students in which higher instruction was given by the masters according to a fixed syllabus and for a fixed time. The student's successful completion of the study program culminated in an academic degree in the arts, theology, medicine or law, which admitted him to the recognized body of masters throughout Christendom. As in any medieval guild the student began as an apprentice studying a particular discipline under a qualified master. As he advanced in his understanding, the student moved to the category of journeyman or bachelor. In the guild system the journeyman had to produce a masterpiece before he was admitted to the highest level in the guild, namely that of master. In the university system the bachelor had to be able to prove that he could teach, dispute and write before he was given his master's license, hat and ring, signs of his authority as a scholar.

For all practical purposes, universities were male communities where all professors and students were classified in the category of clerics. Most of the universities were granted charters of responsibilities and privileges by the Church and became self-governing entities within medieval society. The universities were major centers for propagating the values and ideals of the Western world as these could be expressed by a common faith, Catholic Christianity, and a common language, Latin. By 1500 there were seventy-five universities in Western Europe, but the University of Paris was always considered the intellectual center of Christendom. Thomas spent most of his adult life either studying or teaching at the University of Paris. Here he studied with Albert, taught with Bonaventure, and engaged in dialogue with the finest scholarly minds of his time.

Thomas and Aristotle

The intellectual awakening caused by the rediscovery of the works of Aristotle and their introduction to the West coincided with the career of Thomas Aquinas and provided the philosophical basis for his revolutionary theological system. The Greco-Roman world found its inspiration in the great philosophical treatises of Plato and Aristotle. The Fathers of the early Christian Church came to rely heavily on the philosophy of Plato in their presentation of Christianity as an acceptable intellectual vision of reality. A chief instrument in the continuance of the significance of Plato in Christian thought was the prominence of his work in the theological vision of Augustine. Plato's world view through Augustine came to dominate the thought patterns of Western Europe.

The works of Aristotle had little influence in the West before the twelfth century, although they were highly influential in the Byzantine and Arabic intellectual worlds. The rediscovery and reintroduction of Aristotle's works came into Western Europe through translations and commentaries by Islamic philosophers, such as Avicenna and Averroes, and the great Jewish scholar, Moses Maimonides. In the thirteenth century these translations and commentaries as well as the translations of the Dominican scholar, William of Moerbeke, deeply influenced the thinking of Thomas' mentor, Albert the Great. Scholasticism, as a movement to use philosophy at the service of the faith, took a new direction with Aristotle's reintroduction to Western Europe. Aquinas would use the philosophical insights of Aristotle to present a systematic view of the Christian faith that offered a different perspective from that of Plato and the early Christian Fathers. At Paris Thomas began a totally new way of thinking about and doing theological reflection on the truths of revelation.

Thomas and Gothic Art

Major developments in Gothic architecture coincided with Aquinas' career at Paris in the mid-thirteenth century. The Gothic masterpiece of the Sainte Chapelle, which King Louis IX of France built to house the relic of the crown of thorns, was built while Thomas was in Paris. Aquinas would have been influenced by the order and purpose of the Gothic style, which visually captured the spirit of the times— a desire for order within a hierarchy. Everyone and everything be-

Dominic *(after the School of Guido of Siena)*

longed together and each had a unique place in which to fit; each part contributed to the beauty and integrity of the whole and made it a completed structure.

In a Gothic cathedral each stone, each piece of stained glass, each statue, each pillar and arch, and each chapel blended into a total vision of material and spiritual reality that offered praise and thanksgiving to the God of glory and light. The *Summa Theologica*, Thomas' greatest theological work, is a kind of literary Gothic cathedral in which each part of the mystery of the Christian faith is so presented and related to the other parts that the whole becomes a marvelous proclamation of the beauty of faith seen by the clear light of reason. Using his own natural gifts and talents, Aquinas constantly used the resources of his time and culture to fulfill his role as a Dominican in accomplishing the teaching and preaching mission of the Church.

Thomas and Augustine

The world-view of Augustine had been the determinative vision of the Christian faith for almost one thousand years by the mid-thirteenth century. Using Aristotle and a carefully nuanced understanding of Augustine, Thomas subtly changed the way that Christians thought about themselves and their world.

Speaking out of his own experience and his desperate need for grace in his conversion from a life of sin to a life of virtue, Augustine had a somewhat pessimistic understanding about the human condition. For Augustine the fall of Adam and Eve from the state of grace through original sin was a cataclysmic event which brought corruption and blindness to every subsequent member of the human race. Thomas saw original sin not so much as corruption but as a negation or incompleteness in men and women because they lacked grace as their bond of union with God. Both Augustine and Aquinas believed that the free gift of God's grace or love was absolutely necessary for human salvation. Augustine saw grace as God's remedy for healing the spiritual blindness and corruption of wounded and sinful men and women. Although Thomas agreed with Augustine that grace healed our sinful human nature, he also taught that grace elevated men and women to a new way of being that perfected human nature and made human beings sharers in the very life of God.

Rooted in the Platonic tradition, Augustine saw the world around him as an illusion and a pale reflection of the real world which was heaven or the City of God. Because the human person was a composite of a heavenly soul and an earthly body, he or she constantly experienced the tensions between body and spirit. Because this conflict existed on the social level as well as the personal level, the Word of God had become incarnate in Jesus Christ to heal human conflicts and brokenness. Augustine used the parable of the good Samaritan as the symbol for his understanding of the relationship between Christ and the human race. As noted earlier, he saw the man who fell in among thieves and was robbed and beaten on the way to Jericho as a symbol for humankind. Christ is the good Samaritan who rescues broken human beings by carrying them to the healing inn of the Church where they will be nursed back to health through the sacraments.

Thomas Aquinas had a more positive view of the created world in which all of reality was naturally ordered to God because all the aspects of creation blended into a total order or harmony. Sin brought disorder to God's plan, but grace not only healed and restored human integrity, it also elevated human beings to a new kind of participation in the divine life. Christ was the healer but also the energizer who built the supernatural order of grace upon the positive realities of nature which God had created. The kingdom of God established by Christ on earth through his life, death and resurrection was already the beginning, the seed, of the full glory of heaven that was yet to come. Although the human person was capable of doing good and practicing virtue as Aristotle had taught, the gift of grace was always necessary to activate the full human potential for good. God granted the grace required for a good and holy life in and through the sacraments as they were places of encounter within the Church between Christ and his faithful people.

The *Summa Theologica*

Aquinas' great work, the *Summa Theologica*, exemplified his ordered and positive world view. He organized his theological masterpiece around the *exitus–reditus* principle, that is, everything comes forth from God (*exitus*) and ultimately everything returns to God (*reditus*). As all creatures had their origin in God so they found their completion in returning to God through Christ.

Thomas divided his *Summa Theologica* into three parts:

Part I—the nature of God and the emanation of all creatures from God.

Part II—the return of rational creatures to God.

Part III—Christ as the way by which rational creatures return to God.

In the development of his theological system Aquinas was highly influenced by the logical, psychological and metaphysical insights of Aristotle. At the same time, Thomas' thought was deeply rooted in the revealed word of God found in the Old and the New Testaments. Among the Fathers of the Church, Aquinas was especially indebted to the theological vision of Augustine. The unique contribution of Thomas to Christian theology was his wonderful harmonization of Aristotelian, biblical and patristic insights into a single ordered presentation of the Catholic faith.

Thomas' Theological World View

The principal themes of Thomas' theological world view could be outlined as follows:

1. Beyond the natural order of the surrounding world, which can be known by reason, there is also a supernatural order of grace which we can know only through God's revelation.
2. Our knowledge of the supernatural order, which involves divine revelation (the word literally means a "pulling back of the veils") from God, is the gift of grace received through faith.
3. Despite the radical distinction between the natural and the supernatural, there is no contradiction between reason and faith because faith perfects reason, it does not destroy it.
4. Reason alone can neither prove nor disprove the supernatural truths of Christianity such as the Trinity because they transcend the power of reason.
5. God's power and providence over the world does not destroy human freedom. Those who are saved are saved through the free gift of God's grace and those who are damned are damned because of their refusal to accept God's grace to lead good lives.
6. Eternal salvation, because it is an act of divine mercy not truly owed to anyone, is a free gift of God's grace.
7. Since the primary reason for the incarnation is the salvation of fallen humanity, there would have been no incarnation had Adam not sinned.
8. The sacraments of the Church are more than symbols; they are truly instrumental causes of God's grace in men and women. Christ is the source of grace and true minister of all sacramental action.
9. The Church, the mystical body of Christ, is the sole custodian of the faith and the dispenser of the sacraments.
10. Eternal life consists in the vision of God granted to the saved, who will be happy forever in the presence of God.

21

Fourteenth Century Christianity

The social history of the fourteenth century is characterized by a tension between the needs of the individual and the needs of the universal society. On the institutional level of the Church, the deterioration of the concern for a universal common good is symbolized in the Avignon papacy and the great Western schism.

The Avignon Papacy and the Great Western Schism

In 1309 Pope Clement V (1305–1314), a Frenchman, moved the papal residence from Rome to the city of Avignon in France. During the Avignon papacy (1309–1377), the Popes lost their universal sense of mission and became particularized or local pastors, puppets of the French king, while claiming universal jurisdiction. The pastoral mission of the Church was increasingly forgotten as the papacy modeled itself on the new nation-states of Europe. The already terrible situation became worse during the great Western schism (1378–1417).

The last of the Avignon Popes, Gregory XI (1370–1378), returned to Rome in 1377 but died shortly thereafter. In 1378 the cardinals who gathered in Rome elected a volatile and unstable Italian archbishop as Pope Urban VI (1378–1389). Disgruntled by his reforming zeal and his fits of anger, the majority of the cardinals elected a second pope, Clement VII (1378–1395), who returned to Avignon. Western Europe was now faced with the dilemma of choosing between two popes, one in Rome and one in Avignon. The resulting schism (breach of Church unity) took on political dimensions as northern Italy, Germany, Scandinavia and England supported the

The Great Schism

Roman Pope while France, Spain, Scotland and southern Italy backed the Avignon Pope. This scandalous situation, which lasted more than thirty years, discredited the Church in the eyes of many. Universal moral leadership was reduced to particular and national concerns.

The Black Death

Between 1315 and 1350 a devastating series of natural catastrophes, such as poor harvests and famine, struck Western Europe. In 1348 the "black death" or bubonic plague invaded Europe and caused the death of over one-third of the population. These natural disasters, with their consequent effects on the population, contributed to a mentality of "survival of the fittest." The question for many was no longer their identity and role within the larger community but rather how they and their families would survive the present catastrophes.

Nationalism

The fourteenth century saw the beginning of the breakup of the political unity of Western Europe, symbolized by the Holy Roman Empire. A new spirit of nationalism, especially in France and England, challenged the role and preeminent position of the universal empire. The kings of the new nation-states also challenged the universal authority of the Church and contributed to the particularism that resulted from the Avignon papacy and the great Western schism.

Nominalism

Within the universities, a new philosophical movement called "nominalism" emerged at the beginning of the fourteenth century. Led by William of Occam (1290–1350), the nominalists taught that there was really no such thing as a verifiable universal (a word or concept attributable to many things) since the only truly existent reality was the individual. Occam also taught voluntarism, which maintained that the acts of God were in accord with his unknown and hidden will and not necessarily knowable by or in accord with reason. Great emphasis was placed upon God's absolute power and unknowable will to which the individual had to submit in obedience.

All these social issues contributed to an emerging fourteenth century world view that was very different from that of the thirteenth. The thirteenth century believed in a harmonious universe where everything in the world, in the Church and in individual nations was ordered in accord with reason. Each person, place and thing had its own proper meaning because everything was organized hierarchically so that each had its own proper place and proper relationship to all the other aspects of reality. The men and women of the fourteenth century looked out upon a world whose principal value was survival and in which the individual looked for some meaning amid chaos, war, the breakdown of authority and a discredited Church.

The Search for God in Fourteenth Century Religious Movements

The magnificent Gothic churches of the thirteenth century had sym-bolized the communal journey of the faith community of medieval Catholicism. In the fourteenth century, as the individual was thrown back upon his or her own spiritual resources, the question of the journey to God was recast as the individual's search for a gracious God.

Mysticism

As a fourteenth century religious movement, mysticism proposed direct contact with God by immediate intuition or contemplation. The goal of mysticism was experiential union with God or an imme-diate apprehension of God in some extra-rational way. As a reaction against the formal and the mechanical in religious experience, mys-ticism emphasized the personal and the subjective. Because of its somewhat anti-social bent, mysticism, in seeking to offer security to the individual as he or she journeyed to God, tended to substitute the validity of personal experience for the reasoned and authoritative judgment of the Church.

Catherine of Siena, Bridget of Sweden and Julian of Norwich

Two women mystics of the fourteenth century, Catherine of Siena (1347–1380) and Bridget of Sweden (1308–1373) exemplified a mys-ticism, centered on the person of Christ, that was remarkably per-sonal and profoundly ecclesial. Catherine was a Dominican lay-woman who was truly concerned about the reform of the Church. Maintaining a universal vision amidst the particularism of the Avi-gnon papacy, she encouraged the Popes to return to Rome and to reclaim their universal pastoral mission. Catherine recounted her visions and spiritual experience in her book, *The Dialogue*.

Bridget of Sweden was a wife and mother of eight who founded an order of religious women dedicated to a life of intense prayer. In later life she moved to Rome and worked with Catherine of Siena to bring an end to the exile of the papacy in Avignon. In England a third woman mystic, Julian of Norwich, dedicated her life to prayer and penance as a hermit. In her book, *Showings,* Julian uses feminine language to speak of the motherhood of God.

In Germany, the leader of the religious movement promoting experiential encounter with God was the famous Meister Eckhart (1260–1327). Trained as a theologian at Cologne and Paris, this great Dominican preacher and spiritual director served the order in various administrative posts. Eckhart was influenced by Bernard, Thomas Aquinas and the neo-Platonic perspective. The goal of religious experience is to become detached from this world in order to find a new unity with the image of God in the depths of one's soul. If the individual wishes to participate in the divine life, he or she must allow the Father to generate the word of God anew in the depths of their being. Only by death to the passing realities of this world and new birth to the word of God can the human person come to his or her true destiny.

At times Eckhart lacked clarity and precision in the expression of his teachings. Consequently, he was finally censured by Church authorities who feared that his doctrines might lead to a kind of pantheism which did not distinguish between God and human beings. A more carefully nuanced presentation of Eckhart's teaching was carried forward by the two great German Dominican mystics John Tauler (1300–1361) and Henry Suso (1295–1366).

Brothers of the Common Life

The Brothers of the Common Life represent an important Northern spiritual movement in the fourteenth century. Founded as a lay community which was dedicated to the pursuit of the spiritual life and education, the Brothers of the Common Life were centered in Holland. The spirituality of the community focused on the reading and study of the New Testament. They wished to imitate the simplicity of Christ and the apostles by living a life modeled on that of New Testament communities.

The *Devotio Moderna* or "Modern Devotion," which encouraged affectivity and the practice of penance, is the lasting contribution of the Brothers of the Common Life to Christian spirituality. The literary genius of the *Devotio Moderna* was Thomas à Kempis (1380–

	1328	1348	
	Wycliffe born	Black Death	

1260	1309		1380
Eckhart	Avignon Papacy		Catherine of Siena dies;
born	begins		Thomas à Kempis born

1471) who composed the enduring spiritual classic, *The Imitation of Christ*. While encouraging believers to experience the presence of Christ within themselves and to live deeper spiritual lives, the advocates of the *Devotio Moderna* at times encouraged an outlook that kept people from fully involving themselves in trying to correct the larger and more complex evils present within society, such as injustice and war.

Mysticism represents a personalized approach to religion which emerges when the Church finds itself confused on the institutional level. The mystic can tend to bypass the need for social reform and concentrate on the search for a personal experience of God. As mysticism was one possible avenue of response to the problems of the fourteenth century Christian world, another was the attempt to engage in a broad program of Church reform and renewal.

John Wycliffe

John Wycliffe (1328–1384) was an English priest who studied and taught at Oxford University. Like many Englishmen, Wycliffe resented a papacy living in France which had to be supported by heavy taxes gathered in England. The fourteenth century's spirit of nationalism in England manifested its full vigor when parliament canceled the annual tribute to the papal curia and called for the clergy to be subject to civil rather than to Church courts.

Until 1378 Wycliffe called for a reform within the existing institutional Church, especially emphasizing the need for renewal of the clergy. He taught that only those in the state of grace could legitimately control property, and that the state had the right to take control of Church property when the leaders of the Church were not virtuous and holy men. As one might expect, the English nobles were very supportive of the teaching that enabled them to seize Church lands in the name of reforming and renewing Christian life. A new phase of Wycliffe's career began in 1379 when he began to maintain that the Pope was not the head of the Church and that the Bible alone was the sole and ultimate authority in the life of any Christian.

Believing that all Christians should be able to read the Scriptures

1415 John Hus dies		1453 Constantinople falls to Turks
1414 Council of Constance		1445 Council of Florence

in their own language, Wycliffe translated the New Testament and the Old Testament into English in 1382 and 1384 respectively. He also began to oppose the idea of transubstantiation, the doctrine that taught that at Mass the bread and wine are truly changed into the body and blood of Christ. In attacking the papacy and the Church's understanding of the Eucharist, while emphasizing the role of Scripture and its personal interpretation, Wycliffe attacked the heart of the medieval Church and paved the way for the Reformation. Although his teachings were condemned, Wycliffe's influence continued to spread through the activity of the Lollards, lay preachers who dedicated themselves to renewing Christian life in accord with his ideas.

John Hus

A Bohemian pastor, John Hus (1378–1415), began preaching Church reform along the lines proposed by Wycliffe. Maintaining the sole authority of Scripture within the Church, he called for the renewal of the clergy and a greater role for the laity, symbolized by their reception of the species of both bread and wine at the Eucharist. Hus combined a strong sense of nationalism and an evangelical enthusiasm as he sought to bring the Church in Bohemia more in accord with the patterns that he found in the New Testament.

John Hus was summoned to the Council of Constance (1414–1417) to explain his theological teachings. Although he was promised safe conduct, his subsequent trial and conviction as an heretical teacher led to his death at the stake in 1415. The death of Hus only served to fan the flames of nationalism in Bohemia, eventually leading to a bloody series of conflicts between Hussites and Catholics called the Hussite Wars (1415–1431).

Conciliarism and the Council of Constance

Faced with the intransigence of the Pope in Rome, Gregory XII (1406–1415), and the Pope in Avignon, Benedict XIII (1394–1422), a group of cardinals called for an ecumenical council that would meet at Pisa in 1409 to end the great Western schism and engage in a thorough reform of the Church. The cardinals, amidst the confusion and scandal caused by the schism, had come to advocate "conciliarism," which is the theory that in a moment of severe crisis within the papacy, the highest power of jurisdiction belonged to the bishops of the Church assembled in a general council, who could act independently of the Pope. The Council of Pisa deposed both Popes and elected a third man, Alexander V (1409–1410), who was quickly succeeded by John XXII (1410–1415). However, Gregory XII, Benedict XIII and many other powerful individuals and nations refused to recognize the council's legitimacy. There were now three Popes instead of two, all claiming to be the legitimate successor of St. Peter.

The lack of recognition given by Christendom to the Council of Pisa led the Holy Roman Emperor Sigismund and the Pisan Pope, John XXII, to convoke a new general council at the city of Constance in 1414. This greatest representative assembly of medieval Christendom lasted four years and was attended by over three hundred and fifty officials. Declaring itself to be the highest authority in the Church and superior to the Pope, the council either accepted the resignation or deposed all three Popes and elected a new Bishop of Rome, Pope Martin V (1417–1431).

Although it solved the problem of the great schism, the Council of Constance raised the new difficulty of reconciling conciliarism with the prerogatives claimed by the papacy. For the next thirty years, Popes and councils struggled with the question until the Council of Florence (1438–1445) reaffirmed the traditional medieval Catholic understanding of papal primacy and withdrew its support of the conciliarist position.

In an era of individualism fourteenth century Christians sought to reform their lives, the Church and their society in a variety of ways. Some responded to the challenges of the times by living a life of deeper prayer and searching for a gracious God. Others despaired of the medieval Church and sought to discard the old institutional reforms and begin anew. Most continued to work within the already established patterns and structures of Christian life, hoping that the reform and renewal that all desired could be achieved by patience and courage.

FOR FURTHER READING

William A. Clebsch, *Christianity in European History* (New York: Oxford University Press, 1979).

Lawrence Cunningham, *The Catholic Heritage* (New York: Crossroad, 1983).

William Fleming, *Arts and Ideas* (New York: Holt Rinehart and Winston, 6th edition, 1980). This book is extremely valuable for all periods of history.

Francis Oakley, *The Medieval Experience* (New York: Charles Scribner's Sons, 1974).

Two articles that influenced our treatment of St. Thomas Aquinas and provide valuable information on his life and thought are:

Thomas F. O'Meara, O.P., "Paris as a Cultural Milieu of Thomas Aquinas' Thought," *The Thomist,* Vol. XXXVIII, October 1974, No. 4, pp. 689–722.

J. A. Weisheipl, "Thomism," *New Catholic Encyclopedia,* Volume 14 (Washington, D.C., 1967), pp. 127–28. The late Father Weisheipl lists Aquinas' key ideas, and it is the basis for our treatment.

22

The Religious Humanism of the Renaissance

The Meaning of the Renaissance

The Renaissance, which occurred at various times and places throughout the fourteenth, fifteenth and early sixteenth centuries, marks the transition from the Middle Ages to the modern world through a rebirth of interest in the values and literature of classical Greco-Roman culture. In a broad sense the term "Renaissance" means an era of cultural reorientation, based on classical civilization, in which the secular began to replace the sacred, the individual became more significant than the community, and the humanistic overshadowed the theocentric as an approach to life. In a more restricted sense, "Renaissance" refers to the literary and artistic output of fourteenth and fifteenth century Italy, which was stimulated by the rediscovery of the treasures of the classical past.

The cultural reorientation can be seen as a series of contrasts between the new Renaissance perspective and an older medieval world-view:

1. A secular and individualistic view of life versus a religious and corporate approach to life.
2. An anthropocentric outlook with the human person as the measure of all things versus a theocentric approach in which God is the measure of all things.
3. An urban commercial outlook versus a rural, agrarian outlook.
4. An experiential approach to knowledge versus a speculative approach to knowledge.
5. Involvement in public and social life as a way of serving God

versus withdrawal to a monastery as the highest form of Christian life.

6. Art as the glorification of the ideals and values of the human patrons versus art as religious instruction and the glorification of God.

Renaissance values are still an integral part of the Western Christian tradition, but they also represent a new understanding of this tradition as it recovered from the upheavals of the fourteenth century and experienced the new opportunities being created by economic and commercial growth.

The Renaissance occurred at a time when increased trade and commerce had brought renewed prosperity to many Italian cities. Within these centers of business and banking, a new middle class, with a reawakened interest in the good life including the arts, was emerging. Increasingly prosperous merchants and bankers became patrons of the arts, and they provided the necessary financial resources for translations, authors, artists and architects to engage in a variety of creative enterprises. The invention of the printing press in the early 1450's became the central technological underpinning for the Renaissance and caused an explosion in the availability of information.

The Italian or Southern Renaissance

As the center of ancient classical civilization, Italy was the repository of both the literary and the artistic treasures of the remnants of the Greco-Roman world. The Renaissance began as scholars came to a renewed interest in the writers of ancient Greece and Rome and a reawakened appreciation of the beauty of the art and architecture which had survived from the classical period. There arose a desire both to recover as much as possible of what remained of the literature and art of the past as well as to create new literature and art based on the forms and patterns of the classical world. The interest of Italian scholars in recovering their classical heritage was aided by the influx of Greek scholars from Constantinople, when that city fell to the Turks in 1453. The desire to secure the most reliable text of ancient manuscripts caused the development of high standards of textual criticism in which several surviving manuscripts were compared to ascertain the author's original text insofar as possible. The invention of the printing press made these newly edited texts of the classics available to a broad range of literate men and women. Influenced by the classics, they in turn produced their own literary works which mirrored the style and themes of ancient authors.

The literary Renaissance was paralleled by an artistic Renaissance. Wealthy merchants sponsored the search to recover ancient paintings and sculpture, and they financed artists and architects who reproduced the ancient masterpieces or provided new creations based on the classical patterns and norms. Fifteenth century Italy in general and the city of Florence in particular produced a dazzling galaxy of painters and sculptors such as Angelico, Lippi, Botticelli, Masaccio, Donatello, Ghiberti, Brunelleschi, Bramante, Raphael, Da Vinci and Michelangelo.

The German or Northern Renaissance

The Italian or southern Renaissance took a different tone and direction than did the German or northern Renaissance. In the south the era of reawakening took the form of classical humanism, while in the north the intellectual and artistic revival concerned itself with religious humanism. In Italy textual criticism was used to produce definitive editions of the Greek and Latin classics. In northern Europe textual criticism was put at the service of the Christian faith to provide the best possible texts of the Bible and the early Church Fathers. Italian humanists hoped for a renewed society in which the individual could obtain the fullest possible development of his or her potential in such arts as speaking, writing, singing, and painting. Northern humanists wanted a reformed society in which the Church and its life more closely approximated the ideals presented in the New Testament and the writings of the Fathers of the Church.

The aesthetic and somewhat secular humanism of the south gave priority to revitalizing the values of the Greco-Roman culture, while the ethical and religious humanism of the north emphasized the values of the Judaeo-Christian tradition. Italian humanists wanted to recreate Athens in the age of Pericles and Rome in the age of Augustus. German humanists yearned for the simplicity of Gospel living in the age of the apostles. Both groups of humanists worked for a strong Christian society, but for the southerners that meant a powerful and cultured papacy in a newly restored Rome. For northerners it implied less formal church structures with greater freedom for the individual to seek his or her own spiritual path to God.

Artists and Writers of the Renaissance

The Renaissance witnessed the emergence onto the stage of history of a number of the most outstanding artists of all time such as Leonardo da Vinci and Michelangelo. Important literary figures like Petrarch and Boccaccio stood at the beginning of the Renaissance in its rediscovery of the classics and were formative for its subsequent development. Philosophers such as Pico della Mirandola and Marsilio Ficino sought to reinterpret the works of Aristotle and Plato in ways that differed significantly from their medieval reception. Renowned political theorists like Machiavelli and Thomas More looked for a new understanding of society as the inadequacies of medieval structures became more apparent. Great biblical scholars such as John Colet in England, Cardinal Ximenez in Spain and Desiderius Erasmus in Holland exemplified the religious dimension that was a characteristic feature of northern humanism.

The Popes of the Renaissance

The fifteenth century Popes were concerned with strengthening the papacy, particularly after the experience of the Western schism and the challenge of conciliarism. They had a vision of a strong universal Church that would once more be the heart and soul of the cultural and civil life of Christendom. In their efforts to gain greater political authority and to establish Rome as the new intellectual capital of the Renaissance world, they became strong patrons of the arts, concerned with establishing centers of learning and with building a city worthy of its ancient pagan and Christian heritage.

Pope Nicholas V (1447–1455) invited authors and artists to Rome to begin the process of re-establishing the Eternal City as the intellectual capital of the world. An outstanding humanist himself, Nicholas repaired a number of the ancient monuments of Rome and gathered many of the works which formed the nucleus of the Vatican Library. Sixtus IV (1471–1484) continued the work of his predecessors by building the Sistine Chapel. Julius II (1503–1513) commissioned Michelangelo to paint the Sistine Chapel and Raphael to decorate the papal apartments. Leo X (1513–1521), son of the great Florentine patron of Renaissance art, Lorenzo di Medici, employed a number of artists and began the rebuilding of St. Peter's Basilica.

The Renaissance Popes were outstanding patrons of the arts who succeeded in making Rome the center of Renaissance life and culture. They were also successful in making the papacy a power to be reckoned with in the political struggles of fifteenth and sixteenth century Europe. However, just as the Avignon papacy represented a loss of universal pastoral vision and a localization of papal authority, so too the Renaissance papacy lost its concern for the universal Church and became identified almost exclusively with the politics of the Italian peninsula. The universal pastoral office of the Bishop of Rome had yielded to the needs and demands of an Italian Renaissance prince.

Desiderius Erasmus

The religious humanism of the northern Renaissance found its greatest exponent in the great biblical scholar, Desiderius Erasmus (1469–1536). As a young man Erasmus entered an Augustinian monastery and received his early education there, but he became discontented with monastic life and chose to become secretary to the bishop of Cambrai. While studying later on at the University of Paris he supported himself by tutoring students in Latin. During a visit to England Erasmus met a number of English humanists such as John Colet and Thomas More. As a result of that encounter, he conceived the idea of bringing the new critical techniques of the Renaissance to bear upon the Bible and the writings of the Fathers of the Church. With this project in mind, Erasmus studied Greek in order to be able to read and to edit the fundamental texts of the Christian faith.

Deeply concerned about the reform of the Church and the renewal of Christian society, Erasmus sought to return to the simplicity of life described in the New Testament. He wrote a parody on the times called *In Praise of Folly* in which he asked for reform by criticizing the clergy and showing that ironically foolishness is the cause of much good. In 1516 Erasmus published a critical edition of the Greek New Testament, which became the basis for subsequent translations into the vernacular languages. As a social commentator, a critic of corruption and a major religious writer, Erasmus influenced

Erasmus of Rotterdam

many of the major figures of his time including Martin Luther. Although Luther invited him to join the Reformation and leave the Roman Catholic Church, Erasmus remained within the ancient Church, believing that it was reform and not doctrinal reformulation that was necessary.

23

The Reformation—
Luther and Lutheranism

The Meaning of the Reformation

The Reformation was a movement of religious reform between 1517 and 1545 that resulted in the creation of national, Protestant Churches, distinct and separated from the Roman Catholic Church. The Reformation took place in Western Europe and was a religious movement that had its greatest impact upon the Teutonic middle class of northern Europe rather than the Latin peoples of southern Europe. The main thrust of the Reformation occurred in Germany, Holland, Scandinavia, Switzerland, England and Scotland.

Christians who identify themselves with traditions of life, doctrine and worship stemming from the Reformation are known as Protestants. This term derives from the Diet of Speyer (a formal, deliberative meeting of German princes and rulers) in 1529 when six Lutheran princes "protested" the re-establishment of Catholicism in those areas that had opted for the Reformation. Protestants understood the Reformation as the reform of Christian life, doctrine, worship and structures in order to return to the vision and values portrayed in the New Testament. Roman Catholics sometimes describe the Reformation as a revolt against the universal Church and an abandonment of the development of the apostolic faith subsequent to the New Testament.

The Background of the Reformation

A number of background issues—social, political, religious, philosophical and cultural—developed during the two centuries that preceded the Reformation. In their own context these issues helped to form a mentality that was conducive to the religious upheavals of the sixteenth century.

The Social Context

The natural disasters of the fourteenth century, such as the Black Death, and the human tragedies such as the Hundred Years' War between England and France, contributed to a sense of social instability and insecurity. The medieval idea that identity came from participation in the life of a community began to recede as concern centered on the survival of the individual amidst the chaos of the times. The late Middle Ages became increasingly preoccupied with the individual as distinct from the community.

The Political Context

On the political level the developing nation-states placed increasing emphasis on the significance of their specific national identities. This spirit of nationalism concerned itself with maintaining each country's own rights and privileges and lost sight of the broader values of international cooperation among the diverse nations of Christendom. Although the Holy Roman Emperor remained as a symbolic figure of an earlier medieval vision of Western Europe, the sphere of his power and influence became increasingly more restricted.

The Religious Context

The Avignon papacy and the great Western schism discredited the institutional Church and its authority for many people. No longer seen as a universal binding force within society, the Church as a universal institution began to yield to the national churches as they occupied a more central role in social and political life. The emerging nation-states such as England and France were always in financial need and resented both the wealth of the Church and the money sent to Avignon or Rome to maintain the papal curia or bureaucracy.

		1492 Columbus in New World		1508 Michelangelo's Sistine Chapel
1469 Erasmus born		1483 Luther born		1517 Luther's 95 Theses

The Philosophical Context

On the philosophical level Aristotelian philosophy, as understood and appropriated by Thomas Aquinas, came to predominate within the thirteenth century world view. Reason, as the governing reality of human life, contributed to an understanding of faith which transcended but did not contradict reason. Reason helped to create an ordered and harmonious world in which every person and thing had its place.

William of Occam (1290–1350) opposed this thirteenth century synthesis and proposed a nominalist and voluntarist philosophical view that came to dominate the late Middle Ages (1300–1500). Occam taught that the created order did not come primarily from divine reason but rather from the divine will. God's absolute power knew no limits, and things were good not because they conformed to reason but because they conformed to God's will. God was absolutely free to do whatever he chose to do and was not bound by anything except his own mysterious plan that seemed to have little to do with reason as humanly understood.

The infinite distance between God's power and the human person meant that human minds simply could not fathom the mysteries of God. All events existed within the incomprehensible will of God, and the human person was obliged to surrender obediently to God's authority. When the Church began to experience corrupting influences, it ceased to be a credible authority for ascertaining God's will. This was true at least for some people. The followers of Occam's voluntarism then shifted the source of authority from the Church to the Bible as it demanded the obedience of the individual.

The Cultural Context

The Renaissance in northern Europe was not only a revitalization of classical learning but also a new appreciation of ancient Christian literature. The art of textual criticism, which had been applied in Italy to the ancient texts of the classics, was applied in Germany to the writings of the New Testament and the Fathers of the early

1521 Diet of Worms	1531 Spanish in Peru	1536 Erasmus dies	1546 Luther dies

Church. The study of early Christian literature led many northern scholars to desire a way of living their Christian lives that more clearly reflected the evangelical simplicity of the New Testament. It was into this complex late medieval world yearning for reform and renewal and the opportunity to start anew that Martin Luther was born.

The Life of Martin Luther

Martin Luther was born on November 10, 1483, in Eisleben, Germany. Both his father and mother mixed affection with strict discipline and hoped that their son would become a lawyer. During the course of his studies at the University of Erfurt, Luther was greatly influenced by the nominalist and the voluntarist philosophy of William of Occam.

A strong religious experience in the summer of 1505 caused Luther to abandon his legal studies and to enter the Augustinian Friars in July, 1505. Ordained to the priesthood two years later, he began his unique spiritual journey, the search for a gracious, loving God. Profoundly conscious of his own sin and unworthiness before God, he could find no peace of mind. Believing that God was angry with him and that he was headed for eternal damnation in hell, Luther tried all the remedies for a scrupulous conscience which the Church of his time offered. He spent many hours in prayer; he engaged in acts of penance and self-denial; he approached the sacraments of penance and the Holy Eucharist with great frequency. But in spite of all his efforts, Luther still felt abandoned by God and without any hope that he would ever attain eternal salvation.

Having received his doctorate in theology in 1512, Father Martin began teaching at the newly founded University of Wittenberg. While lecturing on the letters of Paul, Luther came to the insight that human beings are not justified before God by their good works but by God's grace operating through faith. He experienced a new kind of freedom as he realized that salvation was not the result of human effort but rather it was God's free gift of love offered to all. Salvation came by grace through faith and not from good works.

In 1517 Luther nailed his famous "Ninety-Five Theses" to the door of the castle church in Wittenberg. In these theses or propositions he advocated the doctrine of salvation through faith alone as the central point of Christianity. The sole authority for his teaching was the Scriptures, which ultimately became the final authority even greater than that of the Pope or any ecumenical council of the Church. In his theses Luther also attacked the teaching of the medieval Church on indulgences.

The Renaissance Pope, Leo X (1513–1521), believed strongly in a sophisticated and unified Church. He decided to rebuild the ancient Basilica of St. Peter's in Rome as the symbol of the papacy at the center of Christendom. To obtain needed funds for his rebuilding project, Leo authorized the preaching of a special indulgence: the remission of part or all of temporal punishment due to sins already forgiven in the sacrament of penance. If people contributed to the building fund and had the necessary spiritual dispositions, they could receive a full or plenary indulgence. A number of preachers, among them the Dominican John Tetzel, enthusiastically took part in this universal fund-raising effort. In preaching the indulgence many preachers failed to emphasize the necessary spiritual dispositions and seemed to be selling cheap grace, thus abusing the role of faith. It was the abuses that crept into the preaching of this indulgence that occasioned Luther's publication of his "Ninety-Five Theses." Because Luther was unwilling to retract any of his criticisms of the institutional Church and questioned the authority of the Pope, he was excommunicated by Leo X in the bull *Exsurge Domine* in 1520. In the following year Luther went into hiding after being condemned and put under the ban of the empire by Charles V, the Holy Roman Emperor, at the Imperial Diet of Worms.

While in hiding at the Wartburg Castle, Luther translated the New Testament into German. Between 1522 and 1525 popular support for the Reformation continued to grow throughout Germany, especially among the nobles and the middle class of the cities. The lower classes also were initially drawn to Luther's ideas and saw in them a call to overthrow the feudal system in the name of Christian freedom. When the peasants of Germany revolted, however, in 1525, Luther, politically conservative and fearful of anarchy, urged the nobles to restore order with bloodshed if necessary. The violent measures sanctioned by Luther caused many of the peasants to turn away from the Reformation and remain loyal to the Roman Church.

The Theology of Martin Luther

Luther emphasized that the word of God found in scripture was the final authority for his theology and for all Christian life. The Bible contained the word of God because in and through it Jesus the Word

Martin Luther

Incarnate came to all. Luther rejected some of the books of Scripture as used by the Roman Catholic Church, such as the Letter of James, because he felt that they did not contain the Gospel proclamation of salvation by faith alone. Scripture as the norm of faith, which surpassed the Church, general councils and tradition in authority, was authentically interpreted by the individual conscience guided by the Holy Spirit and the Lutheran confessional writings.

In the tradition of Augustine, Luther believed that human beings were so corrupted and depraved because of original sin that they were incapable of doing any good in and of themselves. Only God's grace through faith could justify sinners. God as a just judge of the human race did not overlook sin, but allowed sinners by faith to be clothed in the merits of Christ. Thus human beings who trusted in God's offer of forgiveness in Christ received the grace of justification while continuing to be sinners. The grace of justification by faith alone is an absolutely free gift of God, and there is nothing that any sinner can do to merit such justification.

The Church was an essential element of the Christian message for Luther, and he believed that it was present wherever the word of God was preached and the sacraments were celebrated with faith. The Church was a gathered assembly of faithful believers in which all were priests by reason of baptism. Although Luther believed in an ordained ministry, the pastors of the Lutheran churches were not hierarchical priests granting access to God but ministers of word and sacrament chosen by the local community. The priesthood of all believers meant that each Christian was to minister to others through fulfilling the duties of his or her own state of life. Luther believed that all vocations were equally pleasing to God, and he rejected celibacy by marrying a former nun, Catherine von Bora, in 1525.

Luther rejected the medieval Church's teaching that there were seven sacraments and maintained that only three sacraments, baptism, penance and the Eucharist, had a New Testament basis. In regard to the Eucharist, Luther opposed the celebration of private Masses and composed a vernacular celebration of the Lord's Supper in which the congregation received both the elements of bread and wine. Luther taught that by reason of the words of consecration, "This is my body," and "This is my blood," the body and blood of Christ were truly present in and with the appearances of bread and wine.

Church and state were two aspects of the same Christian society for Luther, but his frame of reference was not the universal Church but the regional churches of Germany or the national churches of Scandinavia. To this day there is a strong identification between church and state in parts of Germany and in Scandinavia.

Lutheranism

In 1526 at the First Diet of Speyer in Germany, it was decided that each prince could chose a religion for his own territory, either the traditional Roman Catholic faith or the teachings of the Reformation, until an ecumenical council could meet to discuss the recent religious developments. Some German princes chose Lutheranism while others remained Roman Catholic. The Second Diet of Speyer three years later canceled the earlier ruling and required that all return to the practice of the Catholic faith. The protest of six Lutheran princes over the demand to universally re-establish Roman Catholicism as the official religion of Germany occasioned the first use of the word "Protestant" to describe supporters of the Reformation. After twenty-five years of struggle, the Augsburg Confession, first presented by the Protestant princes at the Diet of Augsburg in 1530, was accepted with reluctance by the Emperor Charles V in 1555 as an alternative option to Roman Catholicism. Each prince could choose either the Roman Catholic faith or the Lutheran faith as expressed in the Augsburg Confession. Lutheranism quickly became an international movement, embracing Reformation Churches throughout Germany and Scandinavia.

Until his death in 1546 Luther remained an important symbolic personage within the Reformation movement, but the vital forces of the new Protestant vision after 1530 were far beyond his control and often opposed to his actual wishes. In his last years Luther became somewhat pessimistic and discouraged about the forms that the Reformation was taking in its various doctrinal and liturgical expressions. Neither a great saint nor a great sinner, but a profoundly religious and conservative Christian theologian, Luther had hoped to remain a Roman Catholic within a reformed Church. The complex social, political, religious, philosophical, cultural and economic forces of his time turned his ideas into new and radical patterns for Christian life and society. Soon the seeds of Luther's reform of the Roman Catholic Church developed in a direction he had never envisioned. The circumstances and personalities of the times led to the breakup of Western Christendom and the creation of permanent denominational divisions that have endured to the present time.

24

The Reformation— Switzerland and the British Isles

The Reformation in Switzerland

Although nominally part of the Holy Roman Empire, Switzerland was an independent confederacy formed by thirteen cantons or self-governing republics. Deeply committed to humanism, to local self-government and to resisting ecclesiastical authoritarianism, the Swiss cantons were early centers of the Reformation. One of the three Protestant confessions of faith presented to the Imperial Diet at Augsburg came from Ulrich Zwingli of the Swiss canton of Zurich.

Ulrich Zwingli

Ulrich Zwingli (1484–1531), as a parish priest, military chaplain and monastery shrine chaplain, used his leisure time to engage in humanist studies, especially Greek. His time as a military chaplain convinced him that the Swiss tradition of mercenary service was a great social evil. Since Zwingli also became opposed to the medieval tradition of making pilgrimages to various shrines, he soon found his chaplaincy at the Shrine of Our Lady at Einsiedeln an impossible ministry. Moving to Zurich, Zwingli became the principal preacher at the largest church in the city. His growing reputation as a preacher enabled Zwingli to end the practice of mercenary service in Zurich. At the same time he was able to convince the city council to pass an ordinance forbidding the preaching of any doctrine not in harmony with Scripture.

Like Martin Luther, Zwingli preached against any religious practice that seemed to offer the possibility of earning salvation. Desiring a reform of the Church based on Scriptures, he taught that any aspect of medieval Catholic life that had no foundation in Scripture should be suppressed. One of the principal targets of Zwingli's preaching was clerical celibacy, and as a result many priests and nuns in Switzerland followed his advice and left their monasteries and convents to marry. The Protestant Reformation introduced into Zurich by Zwingli between 1523 and 1525 led five Catholic cantons to form a defensive league. In 1531 the Catholic cantons attacked Zurich and Zwingli was killed in the battle which ensued. The Peace of Kappel, which ended the struggle, allowed each canton to chose either to remain Roman Catholic or to opt for the Reformation.

The Protestant Reformation in Switzerland, inaugurated by Zwingli, was much more radical than the reforms proposed by Luther in Germany. While Luther accepted any practice not explicitly contrary to the Scriptures, Zwingli demanded that any practice had to be explicitly mentioned in Scripture to be an acceptable aspect of the Christian faith. Emphasizing the importance of the word of God and preaching in worship, Zwingli rejected the real presence of Christ in the Eucharist and taught that the Lord's Supper was a simple commemoration that enabled the Christian community to remember Jesus' saving work. The teaching of Zwingli, joined with that of Calvin, defined the Reformed tradition of the Reformation, distinct from the Lutheran tradition.

John Calvin

John Calvin was the foremost theologian of the second generation of Protestant reformers. A very careful thinker, he sought to organize the teachings of the Reformation into a coherent system of doctrine.

Born in France on July 10, 1509, Calvin came from a middle class family. After some initial study of theology at the University of Paris, he went on to finish a law degree at the University of Orleans. Calvin began to work in the humanities, studying Greek and Hebrew, at the conclusion of his legal studies. In 1534 Calvin was converted to the principles of the Reformation, and had to leave France because the government was persecuting Protestants. While Luther remained the prophet of the Reformation, Calvin was to become its great organizer.

At Basel, Switzerland, his place of exile, the twenty-six year old Calvin dedicated himself to the study of Scripture. In 1536 he pub-

John Calvin

lished his principal theological work, *The Institutes of the Christian Religion,* as a systematic presentation of the Christian faith from the perspective of the Reformation. This brilliant defense of Protestantism was enormously successful and went through many editions.

After an initial disappointing period of time spent in Geneva, Switzerland, and a sojourn in Strasbourg, Calvin was recalled to Geneva in 1541 by the city fathers. He spent the rest of his life (1541–1564) in Geneva, transforming it into the ideal Protestant city, where religion controlled and dictated the lives of its citizens.

In his theology Calvin emphasized the absolute sovereignty of God and the concept that all things were created to glorify God. Like Luther, he believed that the human person was totally corrupted and depraved by original sin and could do nothing to merit salvation. For Calvin one was saved by reason of God's inscrutable election of the individual, known as predestination, or lost by God's just rejection of the sinner, known as reprobation. The saving work of

Christ applied only to those whom God had predestined to salvation. Since God's actual choice of the individual by predestination to heaven or rejection of the sinner by reprobation to hell was hidden, Christians had to trust in God's promises and be obedient to God's will, as expressed in the commandments, hoping that they were among the elect.

Calvin affirmed a real presence of Christ in the Eucharist, but it was neither the physical presence maintained by Luther nor the symbolic presence taught by Zwingli, but a spiritual presence by which Christ came to abide anew in the hearts of the redeemed through faith. Christian life was maintained for Calvin by three divinely established institutions: the Church, the two sacraments of baptism and the Eucharist, and the civil government. The Church was responsible through its pastors to preach the word of God and to celebrate the sacraments. The civil government had the duty of defending the Church, protecting it from false doctrine and punishing those who were guilty of heresy or immoral lives. The Protestant tradition of theology stemming from Calvin is known either as the Reformed tradition or the Presbyterian tradition, which refers to the system of Church government worked out by the great reformer of Geneva.

The Calvinist work ethic has had an important role in the development of Western European attitudes toward business and finance. Calvin believed that time itself was a precious gift of God that called human beings to work productively and enthusiastically. The profits gained by hard work and thrift were not to be used for enjoyment but were for charity or reinvestment. For Calvin economic success was a sign of God's blessing and a probable indication, if accompanied by a good Christian life, that one was among those predestined to heaven.

The Reformation in the British Isles

The Reformation in England

The influence of the fourteenth century religious thinker John Wycliffe persisted throughout the fifteenth century in England insofar as he had emphasized the role of Scripture in Christian life and a personal relationship to Christ as the basis of lay piety. The rise of national feelings in England promoted a certain reserve toward Rome and the authority of the Pope. When there were many economic and social needs at home, the English Church resented sending vast sums of money abroad to finance the elaborate building programs and military expeditions of the Renaissance papacy. Humanistic studies at the Universities of Oxford and Cambridge promoted biblical research and vernacular translations of the Scriptures as well as advocating the reform of the Church.

Thus King Henry VIII (1509–1547) found strong support among the English people when he broke with Rome over the question of his divorce from his first wife, Catherine of Aragon. The beginning of the Reformation in England can be dated then at 1534 when Henry VIII declared himself to be the "supreme and only head of the Church of England." Between 1535 and 1540 Henry suppressed all the monasteries and convents in England and distributed their lands to the nobles. Everyone in England was required to take an oath of loyalty to Henry as the true head of the Anglican or English Church.

The full impact of the continental Reformation came to England during the six year reign of Henry's only son, Edward VI (1547–1553). When the frail sixteen year old Edward died in 1553, he was succeeded by his half-sister Mary, the daughter of Henry and Catherine of Aragon. Although Mary (1553–1558) was a fervent Catholic who restored relations with Rome and sought to undo the Reformation, she was unsuccessful in her efforts. When Elizabeth I (1558–1603), half-sister of Mary and daughter of Henry VIII and his second wife, Anne Boleyn, became queen, she restored the reforming program begun under Edward and completed the process of making England a Protestant nation. The *Book of Common Prayer,* composed by the Protestant archbishop of Canterbury, Thomas Cranmer in 1549, became the official book of worship for the Anglican Church. The *Thirty-Nine Articles* published in 1563 became the Anglican profession of faith comparable to the Augsburg Confession for the Lutheran tradition.

Pope Pius V (1566–1572) excommunicated Elizabeth and declared her deposed as queen of England in 1570. She showed her disdain for the papacy by inaugurating a fierce persecution of those who remained Catholic. In 1588 Philip II of Spain (1556–1598) sent a great fleet, the Spanish Armada, to conquer England and force Elizabeth to reunite her people to the Roman Catholic Church. The great armada was destroyed off the coast of England by a combination of storms and skillful English sailors. Under Elizabeth and her successors England remained a Protestant nation firmly committed to the principles of the Reformation.

The Protestant Reformation

The Reformation in Scotland

The Reformation in Scotland had a strong political tone with the conflict between Mary, Queen of Scots (1542–1587) and the fiery Protestant John Knox (1513–1572). The middle class under the leadership of Knox united against the crown to introduce the Reformation into Scotland. In 1560 Knox convinced the Scottish Parliament to reject the authority of the Pope and to declare the Mass illegal as a form of Christian worship.

Heavily influenced by the reforming ideas of John Calvin, Knox introduced a Presbyterian form of church government into Scotland. In a Presbyterian form of church government elected lay elders are co-responsible with ordained ministers in maintaining the spiritual discipline of the Church. This form of church polity stands in contrast to an Episcopalian form of church government in which authority resides with a body of bishops, who are understood to be the successors of the apostles. Within the British Isles both England and Scotland became Protestant, but the Anglican Church opted for the Episcopal form of church polity while the Scottish Church chose the Presbyterian form of church government. By 1592 Presbyterianism had become the official religion of Scotland and the Reformed or Calvinist tradition of the Reformation was the basis for Christian life.

Ireland and the Reformation

In 1557 England confiscated large quantities of Irish land and granted it to English settlers as a punishment for Ireland's attempt to free itself from English control. Elizabeth I (1558–1603) introduced the Reformation into Ireland and created a Protestant Church of Ireland, but the bulk of the population, under severe penalties and ongoing persecution, remained staunchly loyal to the Roman Catholic Church.

The English King, James I (1603–1625), colonized Northern Ireland with Scottish Presbyterians. Ulster County in northern Ireland became the center of a strong Protestant minority. The tensions between the Protestant minority, loyal to England, and the Catholic majority which began during the period of the Reformation, have continued with great ferocity to the present time.

25

Catholic Renewal

By the year 1545 national Protestant Churches were firmly planted in Scandinavia, England and Scotland, and regional Protestant Churches existed in Germany, Switzerland, the Netherlands and parts of France. The Roman Catholic Church addressed the Reformation on a variety of levels with its own program of reform. In fact, the Catholic Church was engaged in forms of renewal even during Luther's lifetime.

Catholic Renewal in Spain

In 1492 Isabella of Castile and Ferdinand of Aragon conquered Granada, the last of the Muslim areas in Spain. Wishing to unite their country and renew the Church, the two rulers enlisted the support of the archbishop of Toledo, Cardinal Francisco Ximenez de Cisneros (1495–1517). The cardinal was concerned not only about the moral reform of the clergy and religious but also about the development of the intellectual life. Deeply appreciative of Renaissance scholarship, he supervised the publication of a Hebrew, Greek and Latin edition of the Bible as the foundation for his renewal program.

Ignatius Loyola and the Jesuits

Every epic of Church history has witnessed the foundation of new religious orders to live the ideals of the Gospel and to minister to people's spiritual needs in accord with the culture of the times. Ignatius Loyola (1491–1556) was a military man, strongly imbued with the sixteenth century Spanish vision of crusading idealism coupled with the value of chivalry. At the age of thirty, while recovering from wounds incurred in military service, he underwent a profound conversion experience through reading the Scriptures and the lives of the saints. Feeling called to a deeper life of Christian service, Ignatius gathered a band of like-minded men around himself and established the Society of Jesus, the Jesuits, in 1534. The Jesuits understood themselves to be a company of soldiers or knights who would freely place themselves at the service of Christ the King and his Church.

Sixteenth century Spanish culture fostered a sense of excellence and was concerned with glory, with living life to the fullest. Ignatius chose as the motto for the Society of Jesus "For the greater honor and glory of God." The Jesuits would be a loyal band of comrades characterized by their total obedience to God, to their superiors and to the Church in the person of the Pope.

Anxious to combat the spread of Protestantism, the Jesuits embarked on a number of apostolates in defense of the Church. One of their principal ministries was the education of the laity, who would be taught to better serve the interests of the Church in their various callings and positions of leadership. The Jesuit educational system not only trained the laity in Catholic doctrine but gave them the fullest possible exposure to the great classics of humanist culture.

Another important aspect of the Jesuit apostolate was aiding the laity to lead deeper Christian lives by the use of the Spiritual Exercises. Ignatius designed the Spiritual Exercises as a rigorous thirty-day program of retreat and spiritual formation. The goal of the disciplined experience of prayer and meditation that the four distinct weeks of the Exercises envisioned was the formation of men and women newly committed to living their lives in greater conformity to and service of Christ the King.

Teresa of Avila and the Carmelites

Besides the foundation of new religious orders, sixteenth century Spain also witnessed the reform of older orders. Teresa of Avila (1515–1582) was instrumental in founding a reformed convent of Carmelite nuns who dedicated themselves to lives of prayer and penance. As a visionary mystic and gifted spiritual writer, she was influential in founding numerous reformed Carmelite convents. Teresa's influence also extended to the men of the Carmelite family, and with the help of another great mystic and spiritual writer, John of the Cross (1542–1591), she established a reformed branch of Carmelite friars, who exercised a very important place in the renewal of Catholic life throughout Europe.

Catholic Renewal in Italy

New Religious Orders

The Oratory of Divine Love was an informal organization of priests established in Rome to foster Christian life among the laity. Many important leaders of Church renewal including Cajetan (1480–1547) and Pope Paul IV (1555–1559) were members of this group. The renewal of Catholic life among women was greatly assisted by the Ursulines, an order of religious women dedicated to the education of young girls which was founded by Angela Merici in 1535. A new branch of the Franciscan Order, the Capuchins, was established in 1529 to preach the Catholic faith in Protestant areas and to engage in missionary work in the new world.

Catholic Scholars

The great Jesuit theologian, Robert Bellarmine (1542–1621), became the outstanding systematizer of Catholic doctrine, who sought to win over his Protestant opponents by his reasoned presentation of the Catholic faith. Charles Borromeo (1538–1584), the nephew of Pope Pius IV, helped to draft the Catechism of the Council of Trent and served as a model to all bishops by his own reforming efforts in the diocese of Milan. Cardinal Caesar Baronius (1538–1607), a brilliant Church historian, published a twelve-volume work, *The Ecclesiastical Annals,* which defended the Catholic position that the Roman Church throughout history has shown itself to be the true Church of Jesus Christ.

Catholic Artists

Giovanni Palestrina (1525–1594) created polyphonic musical compositions which served to enrich and beautify the Church's liturgy. His numerous Masses and motets provided the Catholic Church with a rich musical presentation of its faith and helped to renew the worship life of the faithful. A new style of art and architecture, the baroque, came to be associated with the renewal efforts of the Ro-

1519–1522 Voyage of Magellan		
1531 Zwingli killed	1542 Francis Xavier in India	1545 Council of Trent opens

man Catholic Church. One of the outstanding leaders of the baroque movement was Gian Bernini (1598–1680) who sought to proclaim the sacramental and mystical dimension of the Catholic faith in his sculpture and buildings.

The Council of Trent

On the institutional level, the Roman Catholic Church addressed the issues raised by the Protestant Reformation when Pope Paul III (1543–1549) summoned the Council of Trent. Meeting in three different sessions between 1545 and 1563, the council reaffirmed the fundamental doctrinal teachings of the Church.

In opposition to the teaching of Luther and Calvin that original sin totally corrupted human nature, Trent maintained that original sin wounded human nature but that it was still possible for God to heal and elevate the human person through grace. Grace was necessary for any good work and for salvation, and as a gift of God it built upon the goodness still present within wounded human nature. The council also declared that good works, which were the fruit of faith operative in love, were necessary for salvation.

While Luther maintained that there were three sacraments, baptism, penance and the Eucharist, and Calvin taught that there were just two, baptism and the Eucharist, Trent reaffirmed the traditional Catholic teaching that Christ had instituted seven sacraments as the means for conferring his grace. The Catholic experience had always been a sacramental experience in which a whole host of visible realities, persons, places and things, were seen as possible sign bearers of the presence of God. Trent maintained that the seven sacraments were specific instances established by Christ in which visible signs were the means of encounter with invisible grace. In its teaching on sin, grace and the sacraments, Trent was profoundly influenced by the theology of Thomas Aquinas.

On the pastoral level, the council called for a reform and renewal of Catholic life on all levels. Bishops were to be model pastors who were truly concerned about the welfare of the people entrusted to their care. To train priests who were learned and spiritual men, the

	1558			1588		1620
	Elizabeth I reigns			Spanish Armada		Massachusetts Bay
1556		1564		1591		
Ignatius dies		Calvin dies		John of the Cross dies		

The Baroque Style of the Catholic Renewal.

council inaugurated a seminary system for the education and formation of the clergy. Pope Pius V promulgated new liturgical books and
a Roman Catechism which contained the basic tenets of the Catholic
faith in schematic form. Pope Gregory XIII (1572–1585) reorganized
the central government of the Church, reformed the calendar and
established twenty-three institutions of higher learning. Pope Six-

tus V (1585–1590) began a vast program of worldwide missionary outreach that was to be one of the lasting accomplishments of the Catholic renewal of the sixteenth and seventeenth centuries.

Roman Catholic Missionary Expansion

In 1517 when Luther nailed his ninety-five theses to the door of the castle church in Wittenberg, Europe was alive to the possibilities offered by Columbus' discoveries in the New World. After Magellan's circumnavigation of the globe, the riches of the Orient were available to the West via newly discovered ocean trade routes. The Roman Catholic nations, Spain, Portugal and France, were pioneer leaders in world exploration, but they were soon overtaken by two Protestant seafaring nations, England and Holland. The early explorative and colonizing efforts of Spain and Portugal were not only occasions for transporting Western culture to new lands but also opportunities to bring pagan peoples into the Christian faith. Exploration and missionary expansion went hand in hand as Spain and Portugal set out with the sword and the cross. In 1494, Pope Alexander VI, by his famous line of demarcation, divided all newly discovered or newly colonized lands between Portugal and Spain. The Far East, India, China and Japan and eastern South America went to Portugal, while the remainder of the New World, especially Central and South America, belonged to Spain.

The Missions of Spain

Spain was the leading naval and colonizing power of sixteenth century Europe, and in recognition of that position Popes Alexander VI (1492–1503) and Julius II (1503–1513) conceded the "Patronato Real" to the rulers of Catholic Spain. By this papal concession, the kings of Spain were the de facto rulers of the Church in the new lands of Central and South America. The royal patronage allowed the king to appoint all bishops and to administer the goods of the Church and to carry out reforms as he deemed them necessary.

Under the auspices of the Spanish government, Franciscan, Dominican and later Jesuit missionaries came to the New World to convert the indigenous peoples. Often living on the same level as the Indians, the missionaries became the protectors of the poor and the defenders of the rights of the conquered in the face of the cruelty and exploitation by some Spanish officials. One of the particular structural evils of Spanish colonization was the *Encomienda* system whereby the indigenous Indian population was entrusted to Spanish settlers, who often exploited and mistreated them. The Dominican bishop of Chiapas in Mexico, Bartolome de Las Casas (1474–1566), spent thirty-nine years pleading with the Spanish government to reform the *Encomienda* system and to treat the indigenous peoples with the justice and charity which they rightfully deserved as human beings.

The Missions of Portugal

Under Prince Henry the Navigator (1395–1460) Portuguese sailors explored the west coast of Africa. The Portuguese had several goals in mind–they were searching for a new route to the Far East, they hoped to find the Christian kingdom of Ethiopia, and they were looking for slaves. On an institutional level they planted the Church wherever they settled in East or West Africa. Although they installed an indigenous bishop in the Congo in 1520, the Portuguese civil rulers and missionaries were more concerned with reproducing their own culture in Africa than in ameliorating the plight of the people.

Because trade was a primary reason for Portuguese exploration, they established forts for the protection of their shipping routes at Goa in India and at Macao on the southeastern coast of China. Jesuit missionaries accompanied Portuguese explorers and colonizers to India, China and Japan. Francis Xavier landed in India in 1542 and began a remarkable nine year missionary career that took him throughout the Far East, including Japan, before he died off the coast of China in 1552.

The success of the great missionary enterprise of the Church was remarkable. The Roman Catholic Church became synonymous with the culture of Central and South America and the Caribbean. However, while the Portuguese established the Church in certain parts of Africa, this vast continent, for the most part, remained impervious to sixteenth and seventeenth century missionary efforts. The ancient and highly sophisticated cultures of India, China and Japan also were affected only to a slight degree by Portuguese and Spanish missionary expansion.

The Protestant Reformation inaugurated a new era in the life of the Roman Catholic Church. While reform movements had developed within the Church prior to Luther, it was his reform endeavors and their broader impact that forced the Church on the institutional level to address renewal in creative ways. The decrees and reform program of the Council of Trent were formative for the Catholic Church for the following four centuries. The men and women of the new religious orders exercised great influence by their apostolic activities in education, health care, the formation of leaders and the development of a lay spirituality. The missionary expansion of the Church brought the Gospel to the New World, to Africa and to the Far East. The renewed Catholic Church of the sixteenth and seventeenth centuries was preparing itself to face the ongoing challenges of the modern world.

FOR FURTHER READING

Owen Chadwick, *The Reformation* (Baltimore, Maryland: Penguin Books, 1964).

Steven Ozment, *The Age of Reform* (New Haven: Yale University Press, 1980).

Lewis W. Spitz, *The Protestant Reformation* (New York: Harper & Row, Publishers, 1985). This book offers a broad survey of the Reformation period with special attention to Catholic renewal after the Council of Trent, the discovery of the New World and the significance of the cultural shifts in sixteenth century society.

Lewis W. Spitz, ed., *The Reformation: Basic Interpretations*, 2nd ed. (Lexington, Massachusetts: D.C. Heath and Company, 1972). This work attempts to provide diverse perspectives on the religious, social, economic and cultural forces operative in the Reformation.

Index